maranGraphics™ ***Learn at First Sight***™
WordPerfect® 6.0 for DOS

maranGraphics Development Group

Distributed in United States
by Regents/Prentice Hall

Telephone: 1-800-223-1360
Fax: 1-800-445-6991

Distributed in Canada
by Prentice Hall Canada

Telephone: 1-800-567-3800
Fax: 416-299-2529

Distributed Internationally
by Simon & Schuster

Telephone: 201-767-4990
Fax: 201-767-5625

SINGLE COPY PURCHASES

Telephone: 1-800-947-7700
Fax: 515-284-2607

maranGraphics™ *Learn at First Sight*™ *WordPerfect*® *6.0 for DOS*

Trademark Acknowledgments

maranGraphics Inc. has attempted to include trademark information for products, services and companies referred to in this guide. Although maranGraphics Inc. has made reasonable efforts in gathering this information, it cannot guarantee its accuracy.

The Microsoft Mouse design is a trademark of Microsoft Corporation.

WordPerfect is a registered trademark of WordPerfect Corporation.

MS-DOS is a registered trademark of Microsoft Corporation.

Hewlett-Packard, HP, LaserJet, and PCL are registered trademarks of Hewlett-Packard Company.

The animated characters are the copyright of maranGraphics, Inc.

Author:
Ruth Maran

Cover Design and Art Director:
Jim C. Leung

Illustrator:
Dave Ross

Screen Production:
Béla Korcsog

Technical Consultant:
Eric Feistmantl

Editing:
Maria Damiano
Judy Maran

Film generated on maranGraphics' Linotronic L-330 imagesetter at 2540 dpi resolution.

Acknowledgments

Thanks to Ted Werthman of Regents/Prentice Hall for his assistance and creative input.

Special thanks to Wendi Blouin Ewbank for her patience, insight and good humor throughout the project. Also to Saverio C. Tropiano for his consultation and expert advice.

To the dedicated staff of maranGraphics including Maria Damiano, Monica DeVries, Eric Feistmantl, Béla Korcsog, Jim C. Leung, Jill Maran, Judy Maran, Maxine Maran, Robert Maran and Dave Ross.

And finally, to Richard Maran who originated the easy-to-use graphic format of this guide. Thank you for your inspiration and guidance.

Table of Contents

INTRODUCTION

A typewriter makes editing your document a difficult task. If you want to make minor changes, you have to use correction fluid. For extensive changes, you may even have to retype your entire document.

A word processor enables you to produce your document in less time and with greater accuracy. Simple keystrokes allow you to edit and check your document.

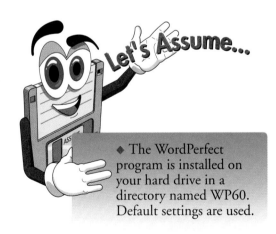

Let's Assume...

♦ The WordPerfect program is installed on your hard drive in a directory named WP60. Default settings are used.

Introduction
Start WordPerfect
Enter Text
Mouse Basics

Move the Cursor
Select Commands
Block Text
Help

What You Can Create with a Word Processor

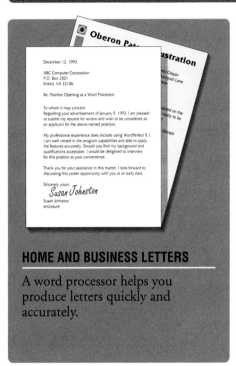

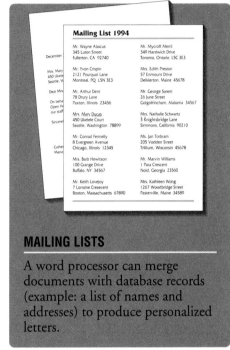

HOME AND BUSINESS LETTERS

A word processor helps you produce letters quickly and accurately.

MAILING LISTS

A word processor can merge documents with database records (example: a list of names and addresses) to produce personalized letters.

REPORTS, MANUALS

A word processor provides features that ease the task of editing and enhance the appearance of your documents.

KEY COMBINATIONS

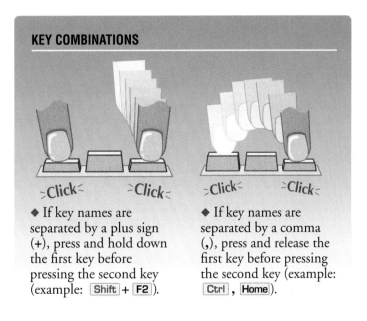

◆ If key names are separated by a plus sign (+), press and hold down the first key before pressing the second key (example: Shift + F2).

◆ If key names are separated by a comma (,), press and release the first key before pressing the second key (example: Ctrl , Home).

START WORDPERFECT ENTER TEXT

Start WordPerfect

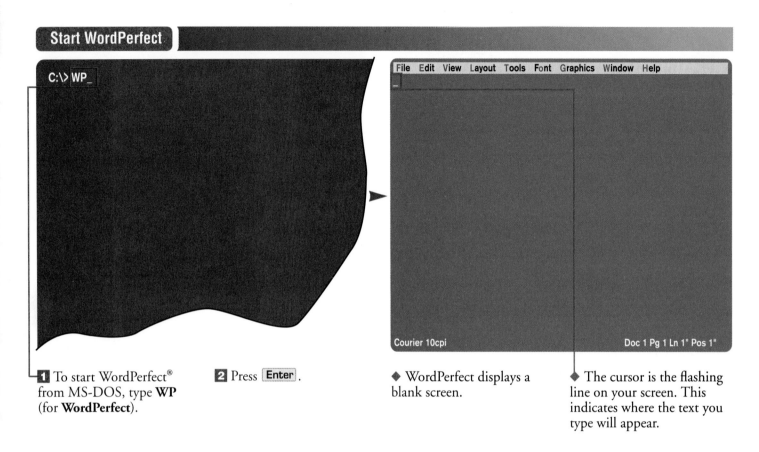

`C:\> WP_`

File   Edit   View   Layout   Tools   Font   Graphics   Window   Help

Courier 10cpi   Doc 1 Pg 1 Ln 1" Pos 1"

1 To start WordPerfect®
from MS-DOS, type **WP**
(for **WordPerfect**).

2 Press Enter .

◆ WordPerfect displays a
blank screen.

◆ The cursor is the flashing
line on your screen. This
indicates where the text you
type will appear.

**The position of the
cursor in your
document is indicated
at the bottom of your
screen.**

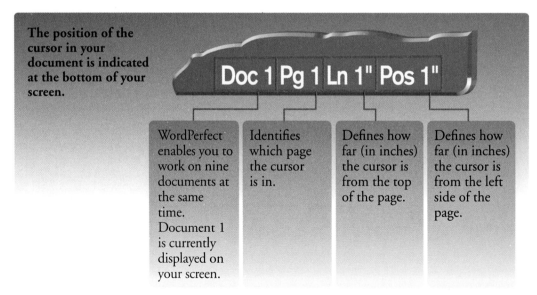

Doc 1 Pg 1 Ln 1" Pos 1"

WordPerfect
enables you to
work on nine
documents at
the same
time.
Document 1
is currently
displayed on
your screen.

Identifies
which page
the cursor
is in.

Defines how
far (in inches)
the cursor is
from the top
of the page.

Defines how
far (in inches)
the cursor is
from the left
side of the
page.

| Getting Started | Edit Documents | Save and Open Documents | Use Multiple Documents | Move and Copy Text | Check Documents | Format Documents | Change Modes | Change Fonts | Tables | Print Documents | Merge Documents |

Introduction	Move the Cursor
Start WordPerfect	Select Commands
Enter Text	Block Text
Mouse Basics	Help

When typing text in your document, you do not need to press `Enter` (or `Return`) at the end of a line. WordPerfect automatically moves the text to the next line. This is called "word wrapping."

When using a word processor to type a letter, the text au...

When using a word processor to type a letter, the text automatically wraps to the next line as you type.

Press `Enter` only when you want to start a new line or paragraph.

Enter Text

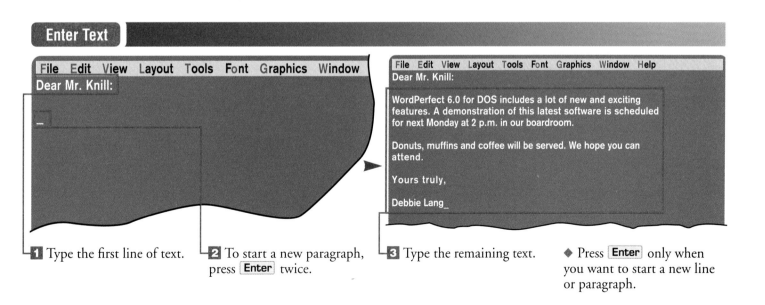

File Edit View Layout Tools Font Graphics Window

Dear Mr. Knill:

_

File Edit View Layout Tools Font Graphics Window Help

Dear Mr. Knill:

WordPerfect 6.0 for DOS includes a lot of new and exciting features. A demonstration of this latest software is scheduled for next Monday at 2 p.m. in our boardroom.

Donuts, muffins and coffee will be served. We hope you can attend.

Yours truly,

Debbie Lang_

1 Type the first line of text.

2 To start a new paragraph, press `Enter` twice.

3 Type the remaining text.

◆ Press `Enter` only when you want to start a new line or paragraph.

MOUSE BASICS

WordPerfect lets you access commands in two ways: using the keyboard or the mouse. Once you become familiar with using the mouse, you may find it faster and easier.

Using a Mouse

Hold the mouse as shown in the diagram. This way, your thumb and two rightmost fingers guide the mouse while your two remaining fingers press the mouse buttons.

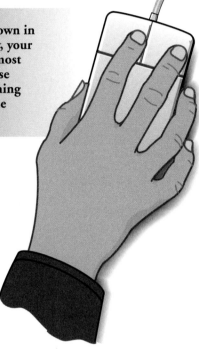

Moving the Mouse Pointer

File Edit View Layout Tools Font Graphics Window Help

Dear Mr. Knill:

WordPerfect 6.0 for DOS includes a lot of new and exciting features. A demonstration of this latest software is scheduled for next Monday at 2 p.m. in our boardroom.

Donuts, muffins and coffee will be served. We hope you can attend.

Yours truly,

Debbie Lang_

◆ A pointer on the screen represents the mouse.

◆ The pointer moves as you move the mouse. For example, the pointer moves down as you move the mouse down.

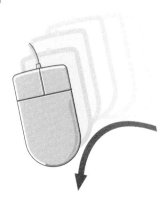

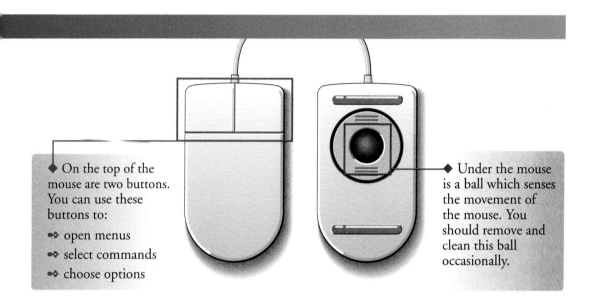

◆ On the top of the mouse are two buttons. You can use these buttons to:

➥ open menus

➥ select commands

➥ choose options

◆ Under the mouse is a ball which senses the movement of the mouse. You should remove and clean this ball occasionally.

Mouse Terms

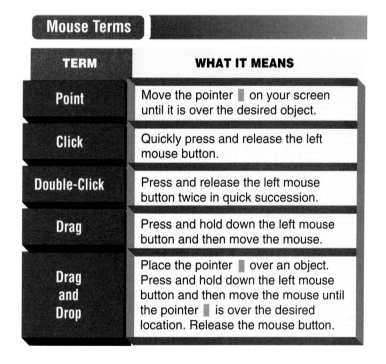

TERM	WHAT IT MEANS
Point	Move the pointer ▌ on your screen until it is over the desired object.
Click	Quickly press and release the left mouse button.
Double-Click	Press and release the left mouse button twice in quick succession.
Drag	Press and hold down the left mouse button and then move the mouse.
Drag and Drop	Place the pointer ▌ over an object. Press and hold down the left mouse button and then move the mouse until the pointer ▌ is over the desired location. Release the mouse button.

MOVE THE CURSOR

Press this key to move the cursor one line up.

Press this key to move the cursor one line down.

Press this key to move the cursor one character to the left.

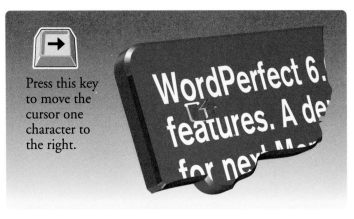

Press this key to move the cursor one character to the right.

Home + **←**	Press these keys to move to the beginning of the current line.
End	Press this key to move to the end of the current line.

Ctrl + **↑**	Press these keys to move up one paragraph.
Ctrl + **↓**	Press these keys to move down one paragraph.

Home, **Home**, **↑**	Press these keys to move to the beginning of your document.
Home, **Home**, **↓**	Press these keys to move to the end of your document.

| Getting Started | Edit Documents | Save and Open Documents | Use Multiple Documents | Move and Copy Text | Check Documents | Format Documents | Change Modes | Change Fonts | Tables | Print Documents | Merge Documents |

Introduction	**Move the Cursor**
Start WordPerfect	Select Commands
Enter Text	Block Text
Mouse Basics	Help

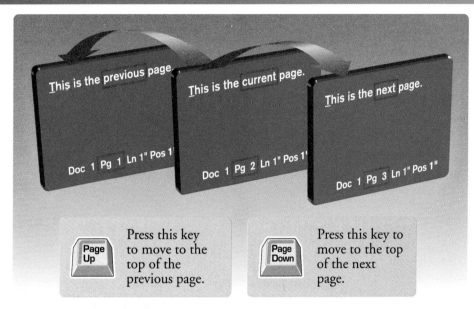

Note: If there is only one page in your document, Page Up *moves the cursor to the top of your screen.* Page Down *moves the cursor to the last character in your document.*

This is the previous page.

Doc 1 Pg 1 Ln 1" Pos 1"

This is the current page.

Doc 1 Pg 2 Ln 1" Pos 1"

This is the next page.

Doc 1 Pg 3 Ln 1" Pos 1"

Page Up — Press this key to move to the top of the previous page.

Page Down — Press this key to move to the top of the next page.

Move the Cursor (Using the Mouse)

File Edit View Layout Tools Font Graphics Window

Dear Mr. Knill:

WordPerfect 6.0 for DOS includes a lot of new and excit
features. A demonstration of this latest software is sch
for next Monday at 2 p.m. in our boardroom.

Donuts, muffins and coffee will be served. We hope you
attend.

Yours truly,

Debbie Lang

1 Position the mouse pointer over the location where you want to move the cursor.

File Edit View Layout Tools Font Graphics Window

Dear Mr. Knill:

WordPerfect 6.0 for DOS includes a lot of new and excit
features. A demonstration of this latest software is sch
for next Monday at 2 p.m. in our boardroom.

Donuts, muffins and coffee will be served. We hope you
attend.

Yours truly,

Debbie Lang

2 Click the left mouse button. The cursor moves to its new location.

9

SELECT COMMANDS

A WordPerfect menu is like a restaurant menu. They both offer a list of options you can choose from.

Select Commands

| File | Edit | View | Layout | Tools | Font | Graphics | Window | Help |

Dear Mr. Knill:

WordPerfect 6.0 for DOS includes a lot of new and exciting features. A demonstration of this latest software is schedu for next Monday at 2 p.m. in our boardroom.

Donuts, muffins and coffee will be served. We hope you can attend.

Yours truly,

Debbie Lang_

KEYBOARD SHORTCUTS

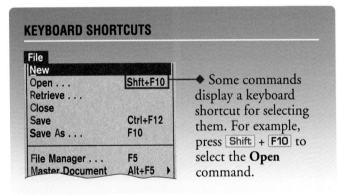

File	
New	
Open . . .	Shft+F10
Retrieve . . .	
Close	
Save	Ctrl+F12
Save As . . .	F10
File Manager . . .	F5
Master Document	Alt+F5 ▶

◆ Some commands display a keyboard shortcut for selecting them. For example, press Shift + F10 to select the **Open** command.

You can pull down a menu to display a list of related commands. You can then select the command you want to use.

1 To open a menu, hold down Alt and then quickly press the highlighted letter in the menu name (example: F for **File**).

 Using the Mouse

❶ To open a menu, click the menu name (example: **File**).

| Getting Started | Edit Documents | Save and Open Documents | Use Multiple Documents | Move and Copy Text | Check Documents | Format Documents | Change Modes | Change Fonts | Tables | Print Documents | Merge Documents |

Introduction
Start WordPerfect
Enter Text
Mouse Basics

Move the Cursor
Select Commands
Block Text
Help

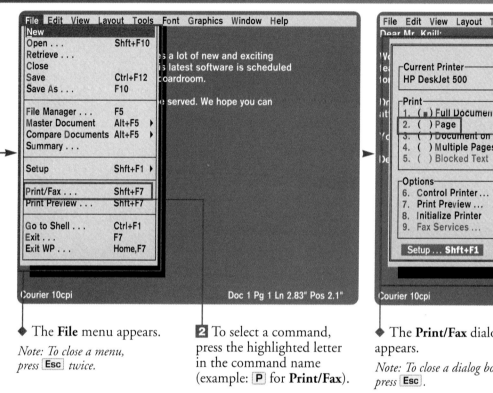

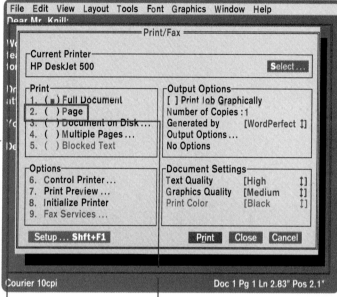

◆ The **File** menu appears.

Note: To close a menu, press **Esc** *twice.*

2 To select a command, press the highlighted letter in the command name (example: **P** for **Print/Fax**).

or

Press **↓** until you highlight the command name and then press **Enter**.

◆ The **Print/Fax** dialog box appears.

Note: To close a dialog box, press **Esc**.

3 To choose an option in a dialog box, press the highlighted letter in the option name (example: **P** for **Page**).

or

Press **Tab** until you highlight the option name and then press **Enter**.

● The **File** menu appears.

Note: To close a menu, click anywhere outside the menu area.

2 To select a command, click the command name (example: **Print/Fax**).

● The **Print/Fax** dialog box appears.

Note: To close a dialog box, click **Close**

3 To choose an option in a dialog box, click the option name (example: **Page**).

BLOCK TEXT

> To perform a command on a section of text, you must first block the text. Blocking highlights (isolates) the text so WordPerfect knows to work with only those characters.

Block Text (Using the Keyboard)

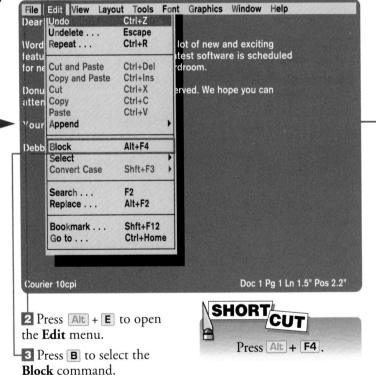

1 Position the cursor on the first character of the text you want to block.

2 Press Alt + E to open the **Edit** menu.

3 Press B to select the **Block** command.

SHORT CUT

Press Alt + F4.

| Getting Started | Edit Documents | Save and Open Documents | Use Multiple Documents | Move and Copy Text | Check Documents | Format Documents | Change Modes | Change Fonts | Tables | Print Documents | Merge Documents |

Introduction
Start WordPerfect
Enter Text
Mouse Basics

Move the Cursor
Select Commands
Block Text
Help

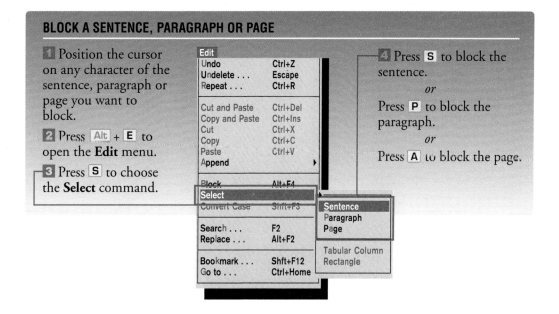

BLOCK A SENTENCE, PARAGRAPH OR PAGE

1 Position the cursor on any character of the sentence, paragraph or page you want to block.

2 Press Alt + E to open the **Edit** menu.

3 Press S to choose the **Select** command.

Edit	
Undo	Ctrl+Z
Undelete . . .	Escape
Repeat . . .	Ctrl+R
Cut and Paste	Ctrl+Del
Copy and Paste	Ctrl+Ins
Cut	Ctrl+X
Copy	Ctrl+C
Paste	Ctrl+V
Append	▶
Block	Alt+F4
Select	
Convert Case	Shft+F3
Search . . .	F2
Replace . . .	Alt+F2
Bookmark . . .	Shft+F12
Go to . . .	Ctrl+Home

| Sentence |
| Paragraph |
| Page |
| Tabular Column |
| Rectangle |

4 Press S to block the sentence.

or

Press P to block the paragraph.

or

Press A to block the page.

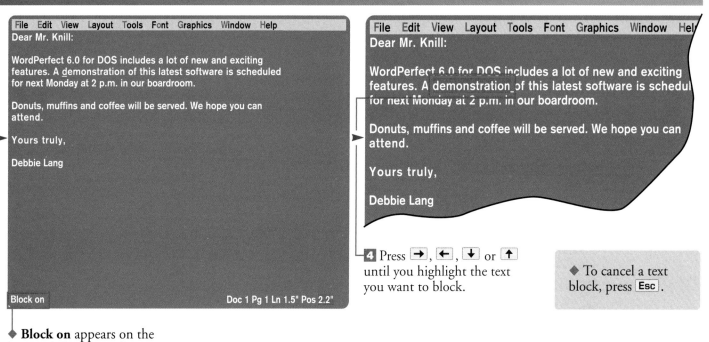

| File Edit View Layout Tools Font Graphics Window Help |

Dear Mr. Knill:

WordPerfect 6.0 for DOS includes a lot of new and exciting features. A demonstration of this latest software is scheduled for next Monday at 2 p.m. in our boardroom.

Donuts, muffins and coffee will be served. We hope you can attend.

Yours truly,

Debbie Lang

Block on   Doc 1 Pg 1 Ln 1.5" Pos 2.2"

◆ **Block on** appears on the bottom left corner of your screen.

| File Edit View Layout Tools Font Graphics Window Hel |

Dear Mr. Knill:

WordPerfect 6.0 for DOS includes a lot of new and exciting features. A demonstration of this latest software is schedul for next Monday at 2 p.m. in our boardroom.

Donuts, muffins and coffee will be served. We hope you can attend.

Yours truly,

Debbie Lang

4 Press →, ←, ↓ or ↑ until you highlight the text you want to block.

◆ To cancel a text block, press Esc.

BLOCK TEXT

You can also block text using the mouse. You may find it easier and quicker to use than the keyboard.

Block Text (Using the Mouse)

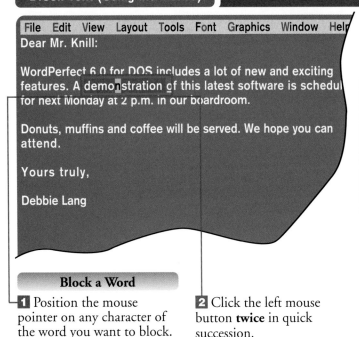

File Edit View Layout Tools Font Graphics Window Help
Dear Mr. Knill:

WordPerfect 6.0 for DOS includes a lot of new and exciting
features. A demonstration of this latest software is schedul
for next Monday at 2 p.m. in our boardroom.

Donuts, muffins and coffee will be served. We hope you can
attend.

Yours truly,

Debbie Lang

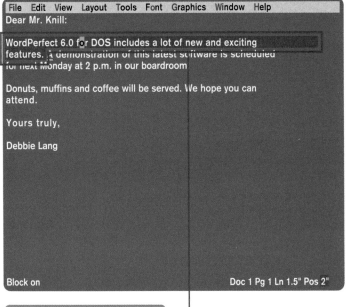

File Edit View Layout Tools Font Graphics Window Help
Dear Mr. Knill:

WordPerfect 6.0 for DOS includes a lot of new and exciting
features. A demonstration of this latest software is scheduled
for next Monday at 2 p.m. in our boardroom

Donuts, muffins and coffee will be served. We hope you can
attend.

Yours truly,

Debbie Lang

Block on   Doc 1 Pg 1 Ln 1.5" Pos 2"

Block a Word

1 Position the mouse pointer on any character of the word you want to block.

2 Click the left mouse button **twice** in quick succession.

Block a Sentence

1 Position the mouse pointer on any character of the sentence you want to block.

2 Click the left mouse button **three times** in quick succession.

| Getting Started | Edit Documents | Save and Open Documents | Use Multiple Documents | Move and Copy Text | Check Documents | Format Documents | Change Modes | Change Fonts | Tables | Print Documents | Merge Documents |

Introduction
Start WordPerfect
Enter Text
Mouse Basics

Move the Cursor
Select Commands
Block Text
Help

TIP

◆ To cancel a text block, click the left mouse button anywhere in your document.

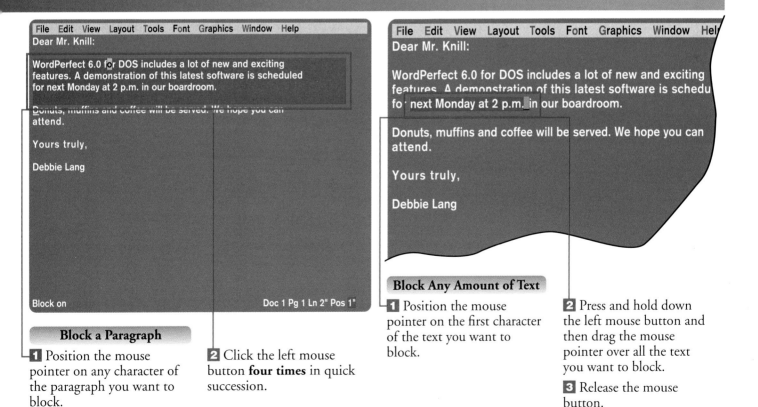

File Edit View Layout Tools Font Graphics Window Help

Dear Mr. Knill:

WordPerfect 6.0 for DOS includes a lot of new and exciting features. A demonstration of this latest software is scheduled for next Monday at 2 p.m. in our boardroom.

Donuts, muffins and coffee will be served. We hope you can attend.

Yours truly,

Debbie Lang

Block on   Doc 1 Pg 1 Ln 2" Pos 1"

Block a Paragraph

1 Position the mouse pointer on any character of the paragraph you want to block.

2 Click the left mouse button **four times** in quick succession.

File Edit View Layout Tools Font Graphics Window Hel

Dear Mr. Knill:

WordPerfect 6.0 for DOS includes a lot of new and exciting features. A demonstration of this latest software is schedu fo next Monday at 2 p.m. in our boardroom.

Donuts, muffins and coffee will be served. We hope you can attend.

Yours truly,

Debbie Lang

Block Any Amount of Text

1 Position the mouse pointer on the first character of the text you want to block.

2 Press and hold down the left mouse button and then drag the mouse pointer over all the text you want to block.

3 Release the mouse button.

15

HELP

If you forget how to perform a certain task, you can use the Help feature to obtain information about it.

Getting Help

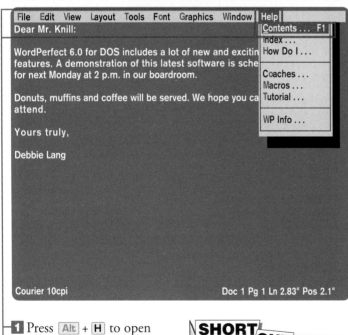

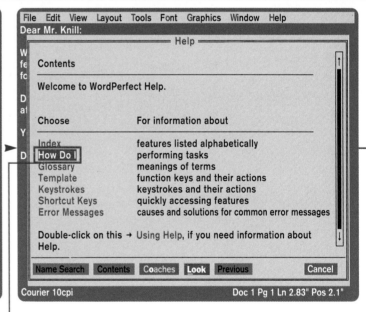

1 Press Alt + H to open the **Help** menu.

2 Press C to select the **Contents** command.

Press F1.

◆ A list of Help topics appears.

3 Press ↓ or ↑ until you highlight the topic of interest (example: **How Do I**).

Note: To cancel Help at any time, press Esc.

| Getting Started | Edit Documents | Save and Open Documents | Use Multiple Documents | Move and Copy Text | Check Documents | Format Documents | Change Modes | Change Fonts | Tables | Print Documents | Merge Documents |

Introduction
Start WordPerfect
Enter Text
Mouse Basics

Move the Cursor
Select Commands
Block Text
Help

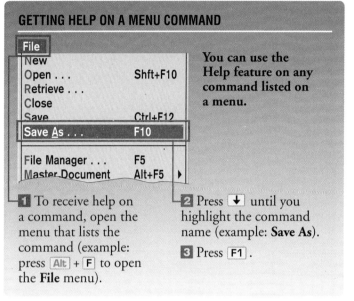

GETTING HELP ON A MENU COMMAND

You can use the **Help** feature on any command listed on a menu.

1 To receive help on a command, open the menu that lists the command (example: press `Alt` + `F` to open the **File** menu).

2 Press `↓` until you highlight the command name (example: **Save As**).

3 Press `F1`.

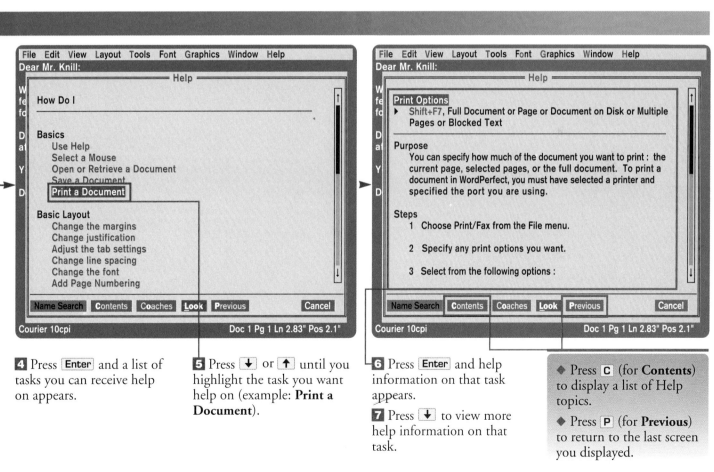

4 Press `Enter` and a list of tasks you can receive help on appears.

5 Press `↓` or `↑` until you highlight the task you want help on (example: **Print a Document**).

6 Press `Enter` and help information on that task appears.

7 Press `↓` to view more help information on that task.

◆ Press `C` (for **Contents**) to display a list of Help topics.

◆ Press `P` (for **Previous**) to return to the last screen you displayed.

INSERT OR TYPEOVER TEXT

WordPerfect makes it easy to edit your documents. You no longer have to retype a page or use correction fluid to make changes.

Insert a Blank Line

File Edit View Layout Tools Font Graphics Window Help
Dear Mr. Knill:

wordPerfect 6.0 for DOS includes a lot of new and exciting features. A demonstration of this latest software is schedu for next Monday at 2 p.m. in our boardroom.

Donuts, muffins and coffee will be served. We hope you can attend.

Yours truly,

Debbie Lang

File Edit View Layout Tools Font Graphics Window Help
Dear Mr. Knill:

WordPerfect 6.0 for DOS includes a lot of new and exciting features. A demonstration of this latest software is schedul for next Monday at 2 p.m. in our boardroom.

Donuts, muffins and coffee will be served. We hope you can attend.

Yours truly,

Debbie Lang

1 Position the cursor where you want to insert a blank line.

2 Press `Enter` to insert a blank line.

Note: The line the cursor is on and all lines below shift downward.

Getting Started | **Edit Documents** | Save and Open Documents | Use Multiple Documents | Move and Copy Text | Check Documents | Format Documents | Change Modes | Change Fonts | Tables | Print Documents | Merge Documents

Insert or Typeover Text
Delete Text
Undelete Text
Reveal Codes

Split and Join Paragraphs

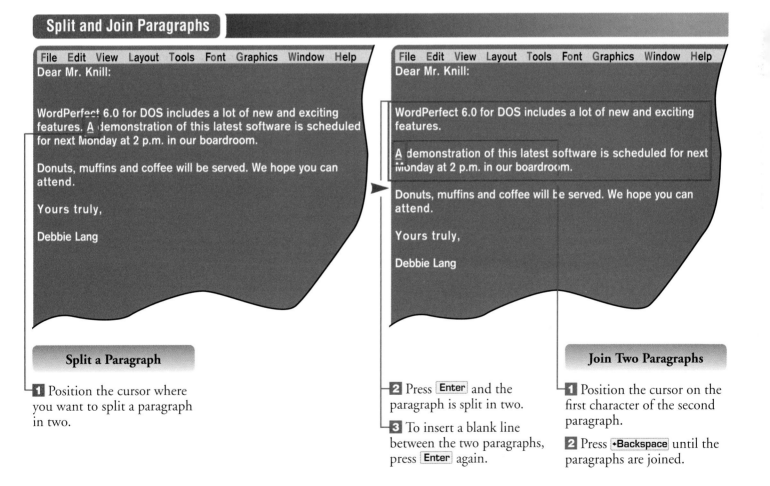

File Edit View Layout Tools Font Graphics Window Help

Dear Mr. Knill:

WordPerfect 6.0 for DOS includes a lot of new and exciting features. A demonstration of this latest software is scheduled for next Monday at 2 p.m. in our boardroom.

Donuts, muffins and coffee will be served. We hope you can attend.

Yours truly,

Debbie Lang

File Edit View Layout Tools Font Graphics Window Help

Dear Mr. Knill:

WordPerfect 6.0 for DOS includes a lot of new and exciting features.

A demonstration of this latest software is scheduled for next Monday at 2 p.m. in our boardroom.

Donuts, muffins and coffee will be served. We hope you can attend.

Yours truly,

Debbie Lang

Split a Paragraph

1 Position the cursor where you want to split a paragraph in two.

2 Press **Enter** and the paragraph is split in two.

3 To insert a blank line between the two paragraphs, press **Enter** again.

Join Two Paragraphs

1 Position the cursor on the first character of the second paragraph.

2 Press **+Backspace** until the paragraphs are joined.

INSERT OR TYPEOVER TEXT

In the Insert mode, any text you type appears at the current cursor position. The existing text is pushed to the right to make room for the new text.

This sentence moves forward as you type.

This is an example This sentence moves forward as you type.

Insert Text

File Edit View Layout Tools Font Graphics Window Hel
Dear Mr. Knill:

WordPerfect 6.0 for DOS includes a lot of new and exciting
features. A demonstration of this latest software is schedul
for next Monday at 2 p.m. in our boardroom.

Donuts, muffins and coffee will be served. We hope you can
attend.

Yours truly,

File Edit View Layout Tools Font Graphics Window Hel
Dear Mr. Knill:

WordPerfect 6.0 for DOS includes a lot of new and exciting
features. A brief demonstration of this latest software is
scheduled for next Monday at 2 p.m. in our boardroom.

Donuts, muffins and coffee will be served. We hope you can
attend.

Yours truly,

When you start WordPerfect, it is in the Insert mode.

1 Position the cursor where you want to insert the new text.

*Note: If **Typeover** is displayed on the bottom left corner of your screen, press* [Insert] *. This turns off the Typeover mode.*

2 Type the text you want to insert (example: **brief**).

3 To insert a blank space, press the **Spacebar**.

Note: The words to the right of the inserted text are pushed forward.

Getting
Started

**Edit
Documents**

Save and Open
Documents

Use Multiple
Documents

Move and
Copy Text

Check
Documents

Format
Documents

Change
Modes

Change
Fonts

Tables

Print
Documents

Merge
Documents

Insert or Typeover Text
Delete Text
Undelete Text
Reveal Codes

Typeover Text

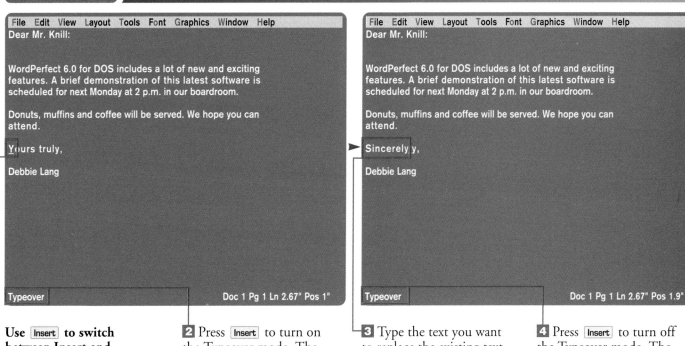

Use Insert to switch between Insert and Typeover modes.

1 Position the cursor on the first character of the text you want to replace with new text.

2 Press Insert to turn on the Typeover mode. The word **Typeover** appears on the bottom left corner of your screen.

3 Type the text you want to replace the existing text (example: **Sincerely**).

Note: The method for deleting the extra "ly" at the end of Sincerelyly is shown on the next page.

4 Press Insert to turn off the Typeover mode. The word **Typeover** disappears from your screen.

DELETE
TEXT

You can delete the character above the cursor. The remaining text shifts to the left.

Delete a character

Delete a caracter

Delete **Delete Characters**

File Edit View Layout Tools Font Graphics Window Hel

Dear Mr. Knill:

WordPerfect 6.0 for DOS includes a lot of new and exciting features. A brief demonstration of this latest software is scheduled for next Monday at 2 p.m. in our boardroom.

Donuts, muffins and coffee will be served. We hope you can attend.

Sincerelyly,

Debbie Lang

File Edit View Layout Tools Font Graphics Window Help

Dear Mr. Knill:

WordPerfect 6.0 for DOS includes a lot of new and exciting features. A brief demonstration of this latest software is scheduled for next Monday at 2 p.m. in our boardroom.

Donuts, muffins and coffee will be served. We hope you can attend.

Sincerely,

Debbie Lang

1 Position the cursor on the first character of the text you want to delete (example: the first **l** in **Sincerelyly**).

2 Press Delete once for each character you want to delete (example: press Delete twice).

Note: You can also delete a character using ◆Backspace. *Position the cursor to the right of the character you want to delete and then press* ◆Backspace.

| Getting Started | Edit Documents | Save and Open Documents | Use Multiple Documents | Move and Copy Text | Check Documents | Format Documents | Change Modes | Change Fonts | Tables | Print Documents | Merge Documents |

Insert or Typeover Text
Delete Text
Undelete Text
Reveal Codes

Delete a Word

Ctrl | ←Backspace

File Edit View Layout Tools Font Graphics Window Help
Dear Mr. Knill:

WordPerfect 6.0 for DOS includes a lot of new and exciting features. A brief demonstration of this latest software is scheduled for next Monday at 2 p.m. in our boardroom.

Donuts, muffins and coffee will be served. We hope you can attend.

Sincerely,

Debbie Lang

1 Position the cursor on any character of the word you want to delete (example: **brief**).

File Edit View Layout Tools Font Graphics Window Help
Dear Mr. Knill:

WordPerfect 6.0 for DOS includes a lot of new and exciting features. A demonstration of this latest software is schedule for next Monday at 2 p.m. in our boardroom.

Donuts, muffins and coffee will be served. We hope you can attend.

Sincerely,

Debbie Lang

2 Press Ctrl + ←Backspace to delete the word.

Note: The remaining text shifts to the left.

Delete remainder of a line

1 Position the cursor where you want the deletion to start.

2 Press Ctrl + End to delete all text from the cursor to the end of the line.

23

DELETE
TEXT

You can delete the blank line the cursor is on. The remaining text shifts up one line.

First line of text

Second line of text

First line of text
Second line of text

Delete a Blank Line

Delete

File Edit View Layout Tools Font Graphics Window Hel
Dear Mr. Knill:

WordPerfect 6.0 for DOS includes a lot of new and exciting features. A demonstration of this latest software is schedul for next Monday at 2 p.m. in our boardroom.

Donuts, muffins and coffee will be served. We hope you can attend.

Sincerely,

File Edit View Layout Tools Font Graphics Window Hel
Dear Mr. Knill:

WordPerfect 6.0 for DOS includes a lot of new and exciting features. A demonstration of this latest software is schedul for next Monday at 2 p.m. in our boardroom.

Donuts, muffins and coffee will be served. We hope you can attend.

Sincerely,

Debbie Lang

---

1 Position the cursor at the beginning of the blank line you want to delete.

2 Press Delete to remove the blank line.

Note: The remaining text shifts up one line.

Insert or Typeover Text
Delete Text
Undelete Text
Reveal Codes

You can delete blocked text. The remaining text shifts up or to the left.

Delete block of <u>t</u>ext

Delete <u>t</u>ext

Delete a Text Block

File Edit View Layout Tools Font Graphics Window Hel
Dear Mr. Knill:

WordPerfect 6.0 for DOS includes a lot of new and exciting features. A demonstration of this latest software is schedu for next Monday at 2 p.m. in our boardroom.

Donuts, muffins and coffee will be served. We hope you can attend._

Sincerely,

Debbie Lang

File Edit View Layout Tools Font Graphics Window Hel
Dear Mr. Knill:

WordPerfect 6.0 for DOS includes a lot of new and exciting features. A demonstration of this latest software is schedu for next Monday at 2 p.m. in our boardroom.

_

Sincerely,

Debbie Lang

You must first block the text before deleting it.

1 Position the cursor on the first character of the text you want to delete.

2 Press `Alt` + `F4` to select the **Block** command.

3 Press `→`, `←`, `↓` or `↑` until you highlight all the text you want to delete.

4 Press `Delete` to remove the text.

25

UNDELETE TEXT

If you accidentally delete text, it is not permanently lost. WordPerfect remembers your last three text deletions and can restore them.

Undelete Text

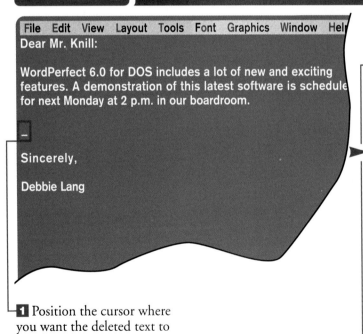

1 Position the cursor where you want the deleted text to reappear.

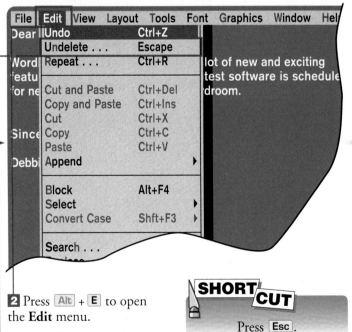

2 Press **Alt** + **E** to open the **Edit** menu.

3 Press **N** to select the **Undelete** command.

SHORT CUT

Press **Esc**.

Insert or Typeover Text
Delete Text
Undelete Text
Reveal Codes

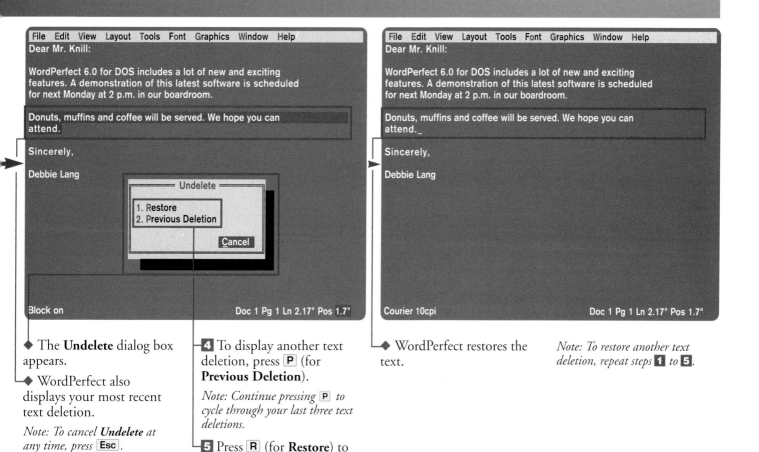

◆ The **Undelete** dialog box appears.

◆ WordPerfect also displays your most recent text deletion.

*Note: To cancel **Undelete** at any time, press* Esc.

�**4** To display another text deletion, press P (for **Previous Deletion**).

Note: Continue pressing P to cycle through your last three text deletions.

5 Press R (for **Restore**) to insert the displayed text back into your document.

◆ WordPerfect restores the text.

Note: To restore another text deletion, repeat steps 1 to 5.

When you make changes to your document, WordPerfect records this information by inserting hidden codes into your document. Displaying these codes lets you see how the program is working. This enables you to edit your document more efficiently.

Display the WordPerfect Codes

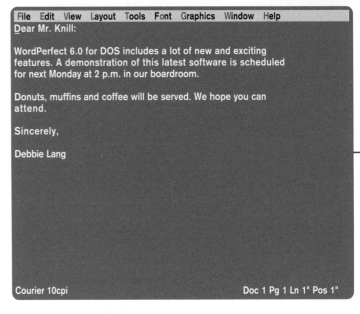

File Edit View Layout Tools Font Graphics Window Help

Dear Mr. Knill:

WordPerfect 6.0 for DOS includes a lot of new and exciting features. A demonstration of this latest software is scheduled for next Monday at 2 p.m. in our boardroom.

Donuts, muffins and coffee will be served. We hope you can attend.

Sincerely,

Debbie Lang

Courier 10cpi   Doc 1 Pg 1 Ln 1" Pos 1"

◆ The codes are currently hidden.

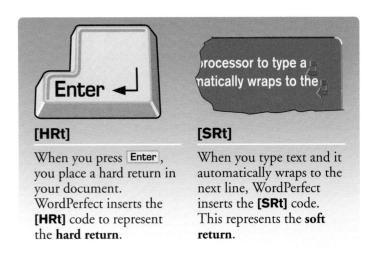

[HRt]

When you press Enter, you place a hard return in your document. WordPerfect inserts the **[HRt]** code to represent the **hard return**.

[SRt]

When you type text and it automatically wraps to the next line, WordPerfect inserts the **[SRt]** code. This represents the **soft return**.

Insert or Typeover Text
Delete Text
Undelete Text
Reveal Codes

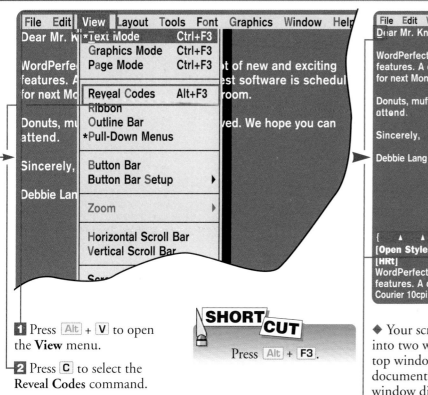

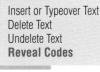

1 Press `Alt` + `V` to open the **View** menu.

2 Press `C` to select the **Reveal Codes** command.

SHORT CUT

Press `Alt` + `F3`.

◆ Your screen is divided into two windows. The top window displays your document. The bottom window displays a copy of your document plus the WordPerfect codes.

3 Press the arrow keys to move the cursor (example: →, ←, ↓ or ↑).

◆ When you move the cursor in the top window, the cursor in the bottom window moves to the corresponding location.

Note: The cursor in the bottom window appears as a red box ( ).

TIP

To hide the WordPerfect codes, repeat steps 1 and 2.

REVEAL CODES

The WordPerfect codes help you edit your document. When you make formatting changes, you are actually inserting codes into your document. Displaying these codes ensures you are making a change in the right place or deleting the correct code.

Insert a Code

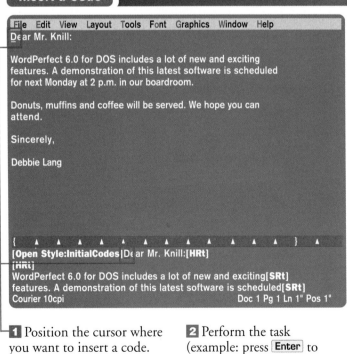

1 Position the cursor where you want to insert a code.

2 Perform the task (example: press **Enter** to insert a hard return).

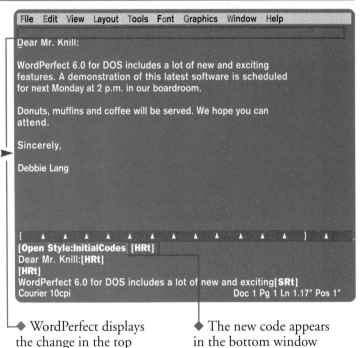

◆ WordPerfect displays the change in the top window (example: adds a blank line).

◆ The new code appears in the bottom window (example: **[HRt]**).

Insert or Typeover Text
Delete Text
Undelete Text
Reveal Codes

Delete a Code

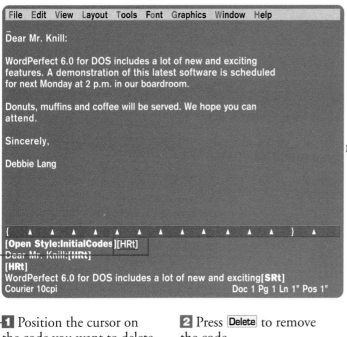

File Edit View Layout Tools Font Graphics Window Help

Dear Mr. Knill:

WordPerfect 6.0 for DOS includes a lot of new and exciting
features. A demonstration of this latest software is scheduled
for next Monday at 2 p.m. in our boardroom.

Donuts, muffins and coffee will be served. We hope you can
attend.

Sincerely,

Debbie Lang

[Open Style:InitialCodes][HRt]
Dear Mr. Knill:**[HRt]**
[HRt]
WordPerfect 6.0 for DOS includes a lot of new and exciting**[SRt]**
Courier 10cpi   Doc 1 Pg 1 Ln 1" Pos 1"

File Edit View Layout Tools Font Graphics Window Help
Dear Mr. Knill:

WordPerfect 6.0 for DOS includes a lot of new and exciting
features. A demonstration of this latest software is scheduled
for next Monday at 2 p.m. in our boardroom.

Donuts, muffins and coffee will be served. We hope you can
attend.

Sincerely,

Debbie Lang

[Open Style:InitialCodes]Dear Mr. Knill:**[HRt]**
[HRt]
WordPerfect 6.0 for DOS includes a lot of new and exciting**[SRt]**
features. A demonstration of this latest software is scheduled**[SRt]**
Courier 10cpi   Doc 1 Pg 1 Ln 1" Pos 1"

1 Position the cursor on the code you want to delete (example: **[HRt]**).

2 Press **Delete** to remove the code.

◆ WordPerfect displays the change in the top window (example: removes a blank line).

◆ The code is deleted from the bottom window (example: **[HRt]**).

Note: To hide the WordPerfect codes, press **Alt** + **F3**.

31

What are Drives?

Your computer stores programs and data in devices called "drives." Like a filing cabinet, a drive stores information in an organized way.

◆ Most computers have one hard drive and one or two floppy drives. The hard drive is called drive C. The floppy drives are called drives A and B.

Hard drive (C:)

◆ A hard drive permanently stores programs and data. Most computers have at least one hard drive. This drive is called drive **C**.

Note: Your computer may be set up to have additional hard drives (example: drive D).

Floppy drives (A: and B:)

◆ A floppy drive stores programs and data on removable diskettes (or floppy disks). Diskettes are mainly used for storing copies of data and for transferring data to other computers. A diskette operates slower and stores less data than a hard drive.

If your computer has only one floppy drive, it is called drive **A**.

If your computer has two floppy drives, the second drive is called drive **B**.

TIP   DRIVE NAME

A: ◆ A drive name consists of two parts: the letter and a colon (:). The colon represents the word "drive." For example, typing **A:** refers to the **A drive**.

What are Directories?

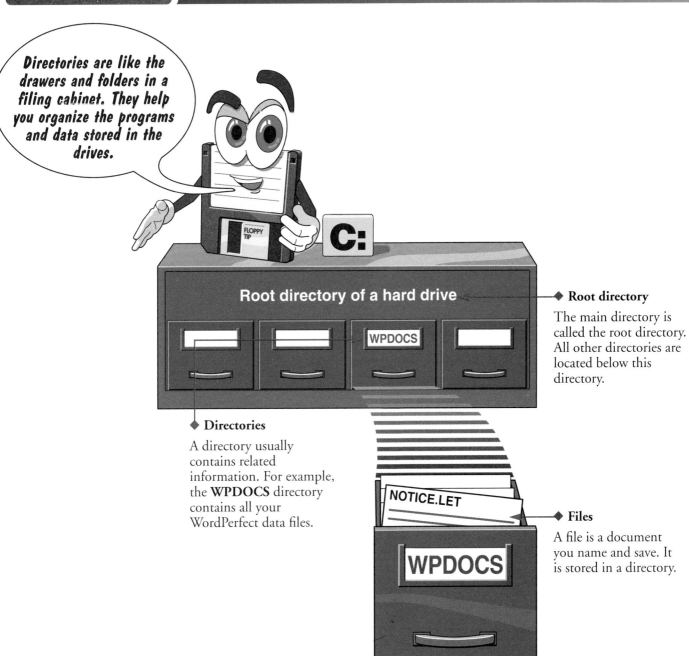

Directories are like the drawers and folders in a filing cabinet. They help you organize the programs and data stored in the drives.

FLOPPY TIP

C:

Root directory of a hard drive

◆ **Root directory**
The main directory is called the root directory. All other directories are located below this directory.

◆ **Directories**
A directory usually contains related information. For example, the **WPDOCS** directory contains all your WordPerfect data files.

NOTICE.LET

WPDOCS

◆ **Files**
A file is a document you name and save. It is stored in a directory.

File Names

A file name consists of two parts: a name and an extension. You must separate these parts with a period.

◆ Period

A period must separate the name and the extension.

◆ Name

The name describes the contents of a file. It can have up to eight characters.

◆ Extension

The extension describes the type of information a file contains. It can have up to three characters.

RULES FOR NAMING A FILE

A file name can contain the following characters:

◆ The letters A to Z, upper or lower case

◆ The numbers 0 through 9

◆ The symbols _ ^ $ ~ ! # % & { } @ ' ( )

A file name cannot contain the following characters:

◆ A period (.)

◆ A comma (,)

◆ A blank space

◆ Some symbols. For example + = | \ / ? < > *

◆ Each file in a directory must have a unique name.

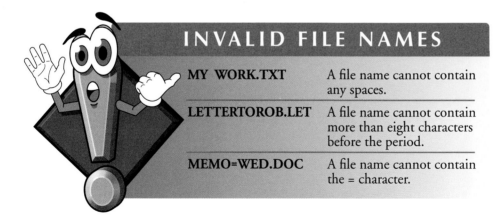

INVALID FILE NAMES

MY WORK.TXT	A file name cannot contain any spaces.
LETTERTOROB.LET	A file name cannot contain more than eight characters before the period.
MEMO=WED.DOC	A file name cannot contain the = character.

Drives   Save a Revised Document
Directories   Close a Document
File Names   Exit WordPerfect
Path   Open a Document
Save a New Document   Find a Document

What is a Path?

If you require a file that is not stored in the default or standard directory, you must tell WordPerfect where it is. A "path" is the direction you tell WordPerfect to follow to locate that file.

IN EVERYDAY LANGUAGE

To locate the NOTICE.LET file, you must:

Find the cabinet labeled **C:** and then

Go to the drawer labeled **WPDOCS** and then

Go to the file labeled **NOTICE.LET**

Go to equals \

IN COMPUTER LANGUAGE

To retrieve the NOTICE.LET file, replace the words Go to with \. Type the following:

C:\WPDOCS\NOTICE.LET

SAVE A NEW DOCUMENT

When you finish working on your document, save it before exiting WordPerfect. This permanently stores your document for future use.

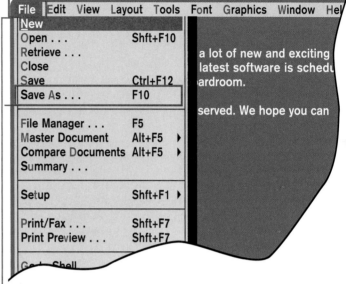

File	Edit	View	Layout	Tools	Font	Graphics	Window	Hel

New
Open . . .   Shft+F10
Retrieve . . .
Close
Save   Ctrl+F12
Save As . . .   F10

File Manager . . .   F5
Master Document   Alt+F5   ▸
Compare Documents   Alt+F5   ▸
Summary . . .

Setup   Shft+F1   ▸

Print/Fax . . .   Shft+F7
Print Preview . . .   Shft+F7

a lot of new and exciting
latest software is schedu
ardroom.

served. We hope you can

1 Press **Alt** + **F** to open the **File** menu.

2 Press **A** to select the **Save As** command.

SHORT CUT

Press **F10**.

TIP ◆ After you save your document, you may want to make changes to it. You can use **Save As** to save the revised document with a new name. This way, you still have the copy of the old version in case you regret any changes you made.

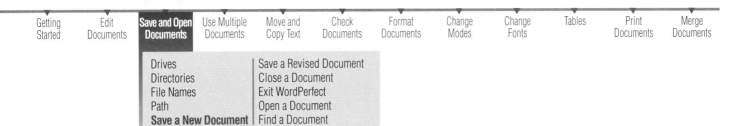

Getting Started | Edit Documents | **Save and Open Documents** | Use Multiple Documents | Move and Copy Text | Check Documents | Format Documents | Change Modes | Change Fonts | Tables | Print Documents | Merge Documents

Drives	Save a Revised Document
Directories	Close a Document
File Names	Exit WordPerfect
Path	Open a Document
Save a New Document	Find a Document

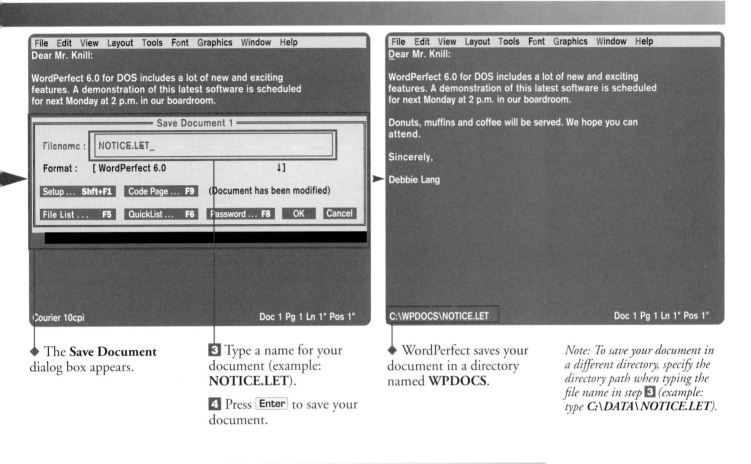

File Edit View Layout Tools Font Graphics Window Help

Dear Mr. Knill:

WordPerfect 6.0 for DOS includes a lot of new and exciting features. A demonstration of this latest software is scheduled for next Monday at 2 p.m. in our boardroom.

```
════════════════ Save Document 1 ════════════════
Filename :   NOTICE.LET_

Format :   [ WordPerfect 6.0                    ↕ ]

Setup ... Shft+F1   Code Page ... F9   (Document has been modified)

File List ...  F5   QuickList ...  F6   Password ... F8   OK   Cancel
```

Courier 10cpi   Doc 1 Pg 1 Ln 1" Pos 1"

File Edit View Layout Tools Font Graphics Window Help

Dear Mr. Knill:

WordPerfect 6.0 for DOS includes a lot of new and exciting features. A demonstration of this latest software is scheduled for next Monday at 2 p.m. in our boardroom.

Donuts, muffins and coffee will be served. We hope you can attend.

Sincerely,

Debbie Lang

C:\WPDOCS\NOTICE.LET   Doc 1 Pg 1 Ln 1" Pos 1"

◆ The **Save Document** dialog box appears.

3 Type a name for your document (example: **NOTICE.LET**).

4 Press `Enter` to save your document.

◆ WordPerfect saves your document in a directory named **WPDOCS**.

Note: To save your document in a different directory, specify the directory path when typing the file name in step **3** *(example: type* **C:\DATA\NOTICE.LET**).

SAVE YOUR DOCUMENT TO A DISKETTE

As a precaution, you should save your document to a diskette. You can then use this copy to replace any lost data if your hard drive fails or you accidentally erase a file.

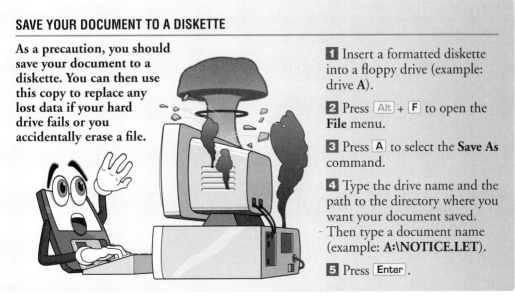

1 Insert a formatted diskette into a floppy drive (example: drive **A**).

2 Press `Alt` + `F` to open the **File** menu.

3 Press `A` to select the **Save As** command.

4 Type the drive name and the path to the directory where you want your document saved. Then type a document name (example: **A:\NOTICE.LET**).

5 Press `Enter`.

SAVE A REVISED DOCUMENT

CLOSE A DOCUMENT

You should save your document every five minutes or after changing a large text block. This protects the changes in case your computer malfunctions or the power fails.

Save a Revised Document

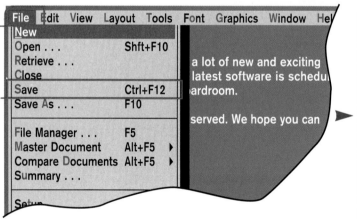

1 Press **Alt** + **F** to open the **File** menu.

2 Press **S** to select the **Save** command.

Press **Ctrl** + **F12**.

◆ The revised document replaces (or updates) your previously saved document.

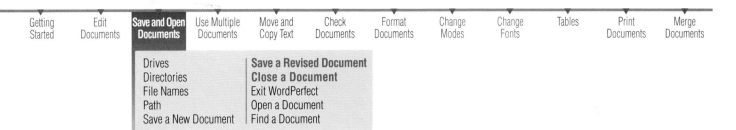

Drives
Directories
File Names
Path
Save a New Document

Save a Revised Document
Close a Document
Exit WordPerfect
Open a Document
Find a Document

Close a Document

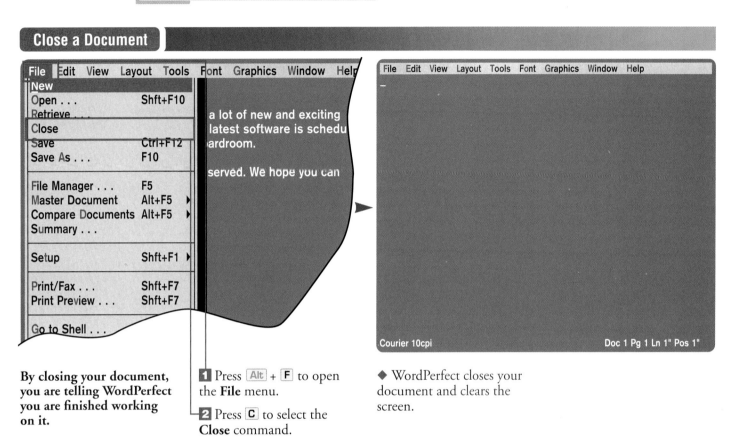

By closing your document, you are telling WordPerfect you are finished working on it.

1 Press Alt + F to open the **File** menu.

2 Press C to select the **Close** command.

◆ WordPerfect closes your document and clears the screen.

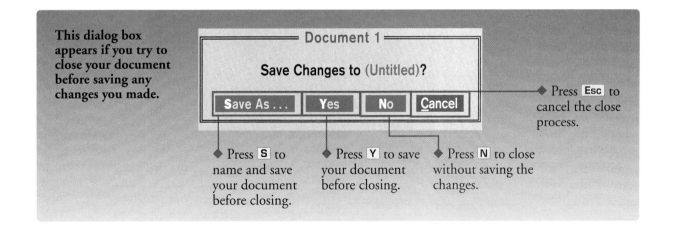

This dialog box appears if you try to close your document before saving any changes you made.

Document 1

Save Changes to (Untitled)?

Save As ...   Yes   No   Cancel

◆ Press S to name and save your document before closing.

◆ Press Y to save your document before closing.

◆ Press N to close without saving the changes.

◆ Press Esc to cancel the close process.

EXIT
WORDPERFECT

Exiting WordPerfect will return you to MS-DOS.

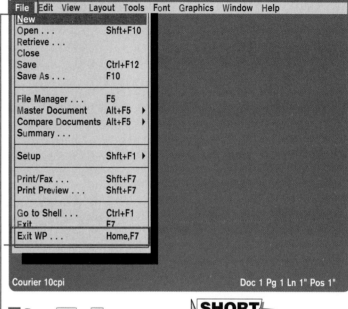

Exit WordPerfect

File	Edit	View	Layout	Tools	Font	Graphics	Window	Help

New
Open . . .   Shft+F10
Retrieve . . .
Close
Save   Ctrl+F12
Save As . . .   F10

File Manager . . .   F5
Master Document   Alt+F5   ▶
Compare Documents   Alt+F5   ▶
Summary . . .

Setup   Shft+F1   ▶

Print/Fax . . .   Shft+F7
Print Preview . . .   Shft+F7

Go to Shell . . .   Ctrl+F1
Exit   F7
Exit WP . . .   Home,F7

Courier 10cpi   Doc 1 Pg 1 Ln 1" Pos 1"

1 Press **Alt** + **F** to open the **File** menu.

2 Press **X** to select the **Exit WP** command.

SHORT CUT

Press **Home** , **F7** .

CAUTION

You must always exit WordPerfect before turning your computer off. Otherwise, files stored on your hard drive may be damaged.

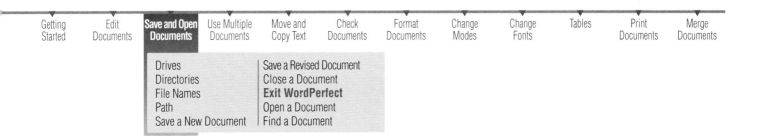

Drives	Save a Revised Document
Directories	Close a Document
File Names	**Exit WordPerfect**
Path	Open a Document
Save a New Document	Find a Document

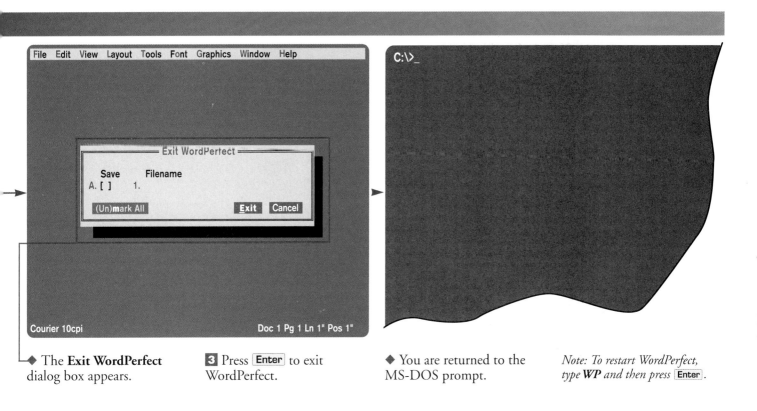

◆ The **Exit WordPerfect** dialog box appears.

3 Press **Enter** to exit WordPerfect.

◆ You are returned to the MS-DOS prompt.

*Note: To restart WordPerfect, type **WP** and then press **Enter**.*

SAVING CHANGES

◆ If an **X** is displayed in the brackets beside the filename, you have not saved the changes you made to your document.

◆ To save the changes and exit WordPerfect, press **Enter**.

◆ To exit without saving the changes, press **M** for **(Un)mark All**. This removes the **X** from the brackets. Then press **Enter**.

*Note: If you want to save the changes, press **M** again to reinsert the **X**. Then press **Enter**.*

OPEN A DOCUMENT

You can open a document to work on it again.

Open a Document

File	Edit	View	Layout	Tools	Font	Graphics	Window	Hel

New	
Open . . .	Shft+F10
Retrieve . . .	
Close	
Save	Ctrl+F12
Save As . . .	F10
File Manager . . .	F5
Master Document	Alt+F5 ▸
Compare Documents	Alt+F5 ▸
Summary . . .	
Setup	Shft+F1 ▸
Print/Fax . . .	Shft+F7
Print Preview . . .	Shft+F7

1 Press `Alt` + `F` to open the **File** menu.

2 Press `O` to select the **Open** command.

SHORT CUT

Press `Shift` + `F10`.

RETRIEVE A DOCUMENT

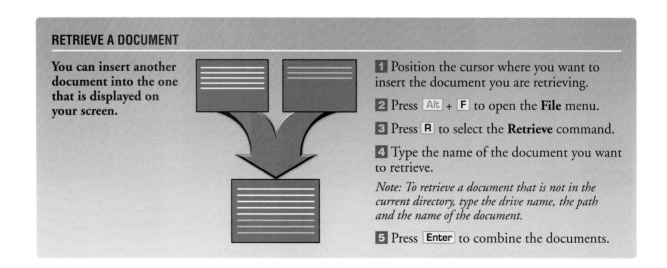

You can insert another document into the one that is displayed on your screen.

1 Position the cursor where you want to insert the document you are retrieving.

2 Press `Alt` + `F` to open the **File** menu.

3 Press `R` to select the **Retrieve** command.

4 Type the name of the document you want to retrieve.

Note: To retrieve a document that is not in the current directory, type the drive name, the path and the name of the document.

5 Press `Enter` to combine the documents.

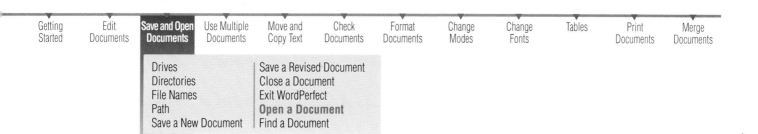

| Getting Started | Edit Documents | **Save and Open Documents** | Use Multiple Documents | Move and Copy Text | Check Documents | Format Documents | Change Modes | Change Fonts | Tables | Print Documents | Merge Documents |

Drives
Directories
File Names
Path
Save a New Document

Save a Revised Document
Close a Document
Exit WordPerfect
Open a Document
Find a Document

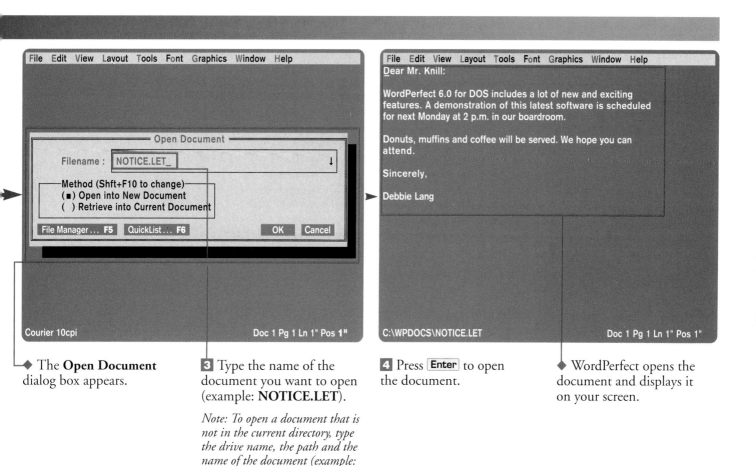

◆ The **Open Document** dialog box appears.

3 Type the name of the document you want to open (example: **NOTICE.LET**).

Note: To open a document that is not in the current directory, type the drive name, the path and the name of the document (example: type C:\DATA\NOTICE.LET).

4 Press **Enter** to open the document.

◆ WordPerfect opens the document and displays it on your screen.

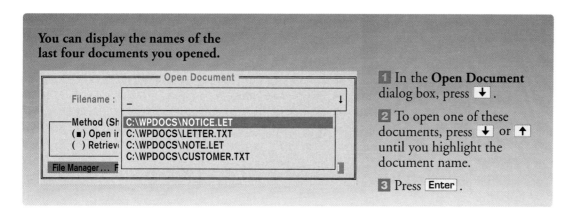

You can display the names of the last four documents you opened.

1 In the **Open Document** dialog box, press **↓**.

2 To open one of these documents, press **↓** or **↑** until you highlight the document name.

3 Press **Enter**.

43

FIND A
DOCUMENT

If you forget the name of the file you want to work on, WordPerfect can display a list of your files. You can then view the contents of each file to find the one you need.

Find a Document

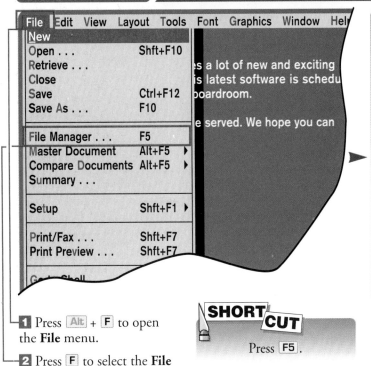

File	Edit	View	Layout	Tools	Font	Graphics	Window	Hel

New
Open . . .   Shft+F10
Retrieve . . .
Close
Save   Ctrl+F12
Save As . . .   F10

File Manager . . .   F5
Master Document   Alt+F5   ▶
Compare Documents Alt+F5   ▶
Summary . . .

Setup   Shft+F1   ▶

Print/Fax . . .   Shft+F7
Print Preview . . .   Shft+F7

es a lot of new and exciting
is latest software is schedu
boardroom.

e served. We hope you can

SHORT CUT

Press **F5**.

1 Press **Alt** + **F** to open the **File** menu.

2 Press **F** to select the **File Manager** command.

File	Edit	View	Layout	Tools	Font	Graphics	Window	Help

Dear Mr. Knill:

WordPerfect 6.0 for DOS includes a lot of new and exciting features. A demonstration of this latest software is scheduled for next Monday at 2 p.m. in our boardroom.

Donuts, muffins and coffee will be served. We hope you can attend.

Sincerel

Debbie L

Specify File Manager List

Directory : C:\WPDOCS*.*

QuickList . . . F6   Use QuickFinder . . . F4

Directory Tree . . . F8   Redo F5   OK   Cancel

C:\WPDOCS\NOTICE.LET   Doc 1 Pg 1 Ln 1" Pos 1"

◆ The drive and path of the current directory appear.

3 Press **Enter** to display the contents of this directory.

*Note: To view the documents in a different directory, type the drive name and the path to that directory (example: **C:\WP60**) and then press **Enter**.*

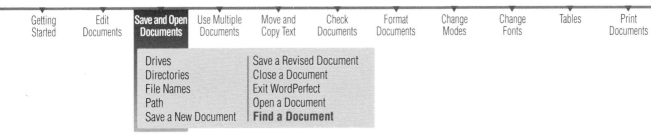

| Getting Started | Edit Documents | **Save and Open Documents** | Use Multiple Documents | Move and Copy Text | Check Documents | Format Documents | Change Modes | Change Fonts | Tables | Print Documents | Merge Documents |

Drives
Directories
File Names
Path
Save a New Document

Save a Revised Document
Close a Document
Exit WordPerfect
Open a Document
Find a Document

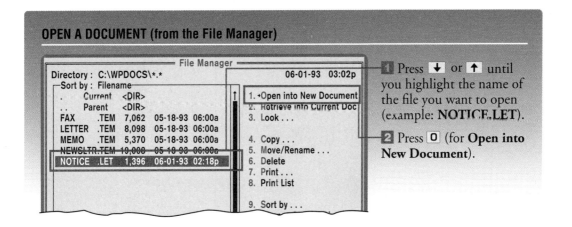

OPEN A DOCUMENT (from the File Manager)

1 Press ⬇ or ⬆ until you highlight the name of the file you want to open (example: **NOTICE.LET**).

2 Press **O** (for **Open into New Document**).

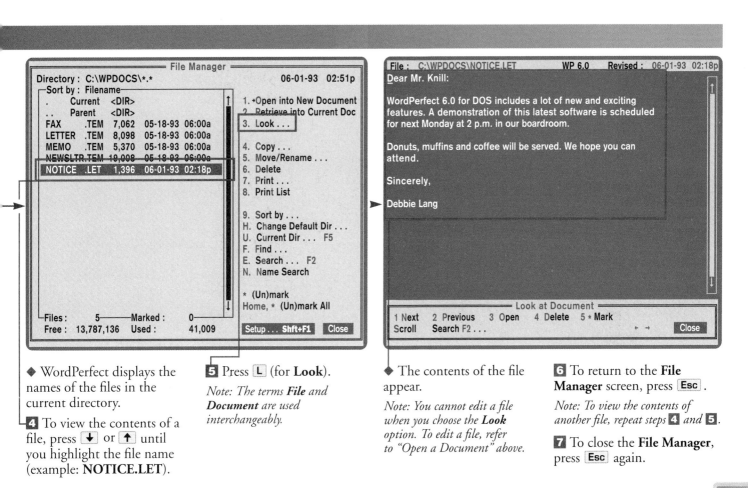

◆ WordPerfect displays the names of the files in the current directory.

4 To view the contents of a file, press ⬇ or ⬆ until you highlight the file name (example: **NOTICE.LET**).

5 Press **L** (for **Look**).

*Note: The terms **File** and **Document** are used interchangeably.*

◆ The contents of the file appear.

*Note: You cannot edit a file when you choose the **Look** option. To edit a file, refer to "Open a Document" above.*

6 To return to the **File Manager** screen, press **Esc**.

*Note: To view the contents of another file, repeat steps **4** and **5**.*

7 To close the **File Manager**, press **Esc** again.

OPEN
A NEW
DOCUMENT

DISPLAY
PREVIOUS
DOCUMENT

WordPerfect lets you work on nine separate documents at the same time.

Open a New Document

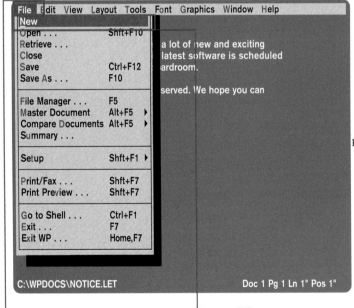

C:\WPDOCS\NOTICE.LET   Doc 1 Pg 1 Ln 1" Pos 1"

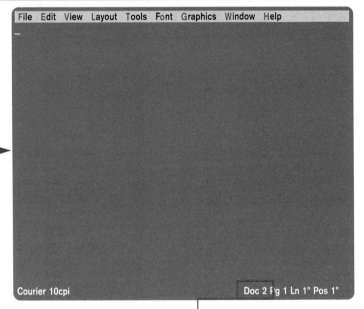

Courier 10cpi   Doc 2 Pg 1 Ln 1" Pos 1"

You can open a new document at any time.

1 Press `Alt` + `F` to open the **File** menu.

2 Press `N` to select the **New** command.

◆ A new document appears.

◆ The document number is displayed on the bottom right corner of your screen.

Note: A document is given a number when you open it. This helps you keep track of the number of documents you are working on.

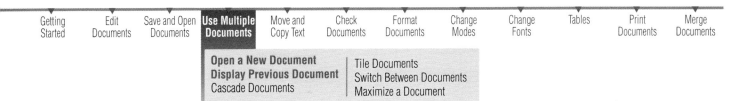

Open a New Document
Display Previous Document
Cascade Documents

Tile Documents
Switch Between Documents
Maximize a Document

Display Previous Document

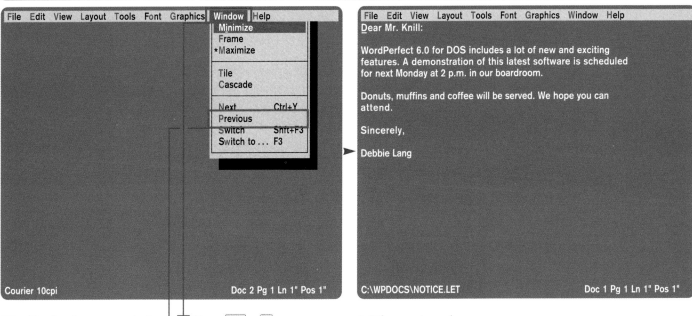

WordPerfect lets you switch between all your open documents.

Note: You can only edit the document displayed on your screen.

1 Press `Alt` + `W` to open the **Window** menu.

2 Press `P` to select the **Previous** command.

◆ The previous document appears.

CASCADE DOCUMENTS

TILE DOCUMENTS

If you have several documents open, some of them may be hidden from view. The Cascade command lets you display all your open documents by overlapping them.

Cascade Documents

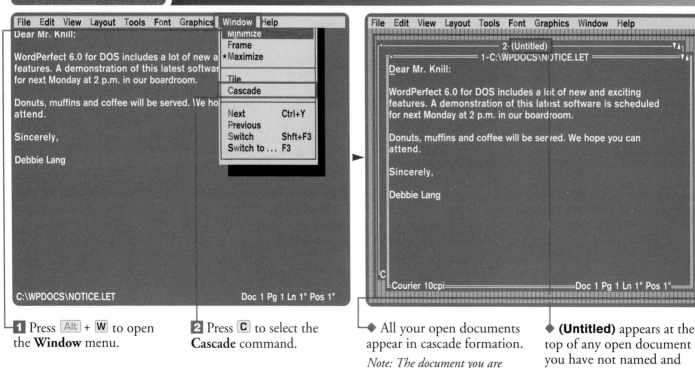

1 Press `Alt` + `W` to open the **Window** menu.

2 Press `C` to select the **Cascade** command.

◆ All your open documents appear in cascade formation.

Note: The document you are currently working on appears in front.

◆ **(Untitled)** appears at the top of any open document you have not named and saved.

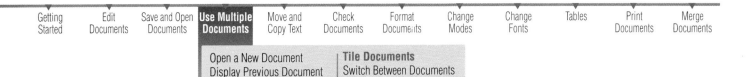

| Getting Started | Edit Documents | Save and Open Documents | **Use Multiple Documents** | Move and Copy Text | Check Documents | Format Documents | Change Modes | Change Fonts | Tables | Print Documents | Merge Documents |

Open a New Document
Display Previous Document
Cascade Documents

Tile Documents
Switch Between Documents
Maximize a Document

The Tile command lets you display all your open documents side-by-side without overlapping them.

Tile Documents

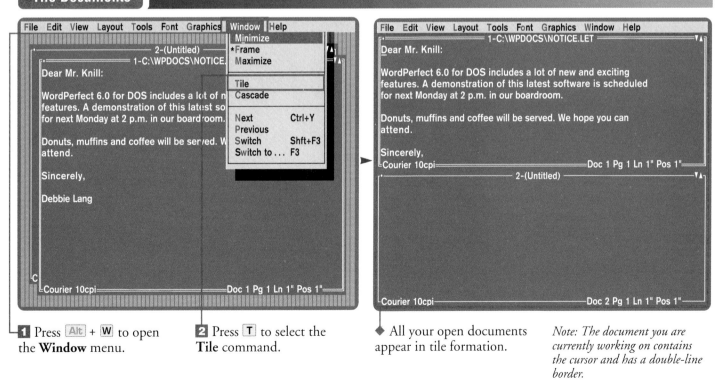

1 Press `Alt` + `W` to open the **Window** menu.

2 Press `T` to select the **Tile** command.

◆ All your open documents appear in tile formation.

Note: The document you are currently working on contains the cursor and has a double-line border.

SWITCH BETWEEN DOCUMENTS

MAXIMIZE A DOCUMENT

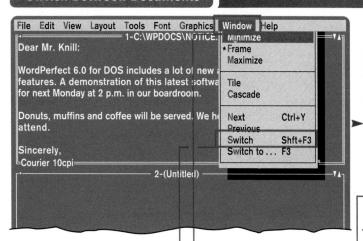

WordPerfect lets you switch between the current document and the last document you worked on.

◆ The current document contains the cursor. You can only edit the current document.

1 Press Alt + W to open the **Window** menu.

2 Press S to select the **Switch** command.

Press Shift + F3.

◆ The cursor moves to the last document you worked on. You can now edit this document.

Note: To switch back, repeat steps 1 and 2.

Using the Mouse

❶ Click anywhere in the document you want to switch to.

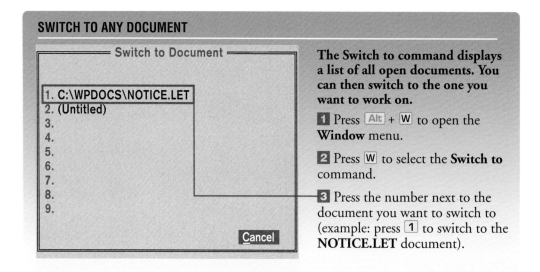

SWITCH TO ANY DOCUMENT

Switch to Document

1. C:\WPDOCS\NOTICE.LET
2. (Untitled)
3.
4.
5.
6.
7.
8.
9.

Cancel

The Switch to command displays a list of all open documents. You can then switch to the one you want to work on.

1 Press Alt + W to open the **Window** menu.

2 Press W to select the **Switch to** command.

3 Press the number next to the document you want to switch to (example: press 1 to switch to the **NOTICE.LET** document).

| Getting Started | Edit Documents | Save and Open Documents | **Use Multiple Documents** | Move and Copy Text | Check Documents | Format Documents | Change Modes | Change Fonts | Tables | Print Documents | Merge Documents |

Open a New Document
Display Previous Document
Cascade Documents

Tile Documents
Switch Between Documents
Maximize a Document

You can enlarge (maximize) the current document to fill your entire screen.

Maximize a Document

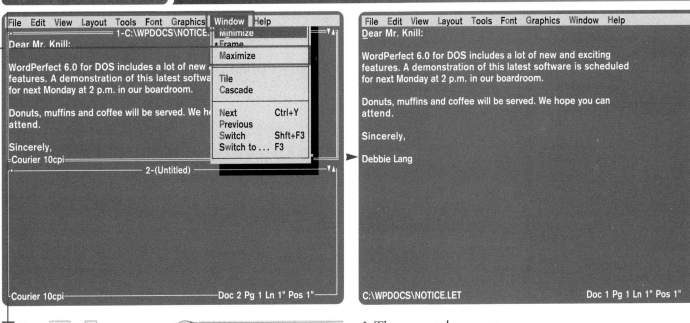

1 Press Alt + W to open the **Window** menu.

2 Press M to select the **Maximize** command.

Using the Mouse

1 Click the maximize arrow ▲ located on the top right corner of the document you want to maximize.

◆ The current document is maximized to fill your entire screen.

You can move text from one location in your document to another. WordPerfect "cuts" the text and "pastes" it in a new location. The original text disappears.

Move Text

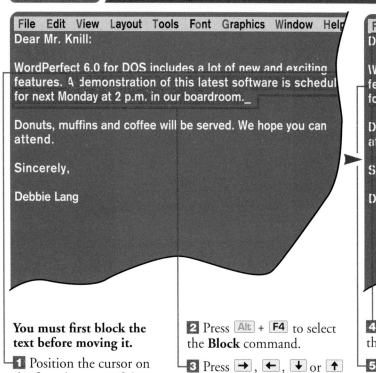

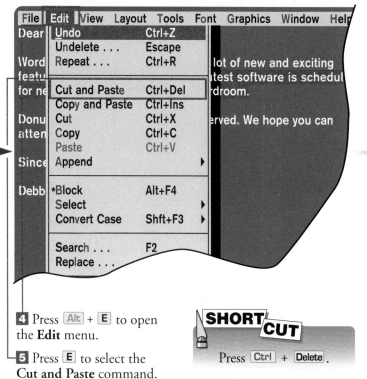

You must first block the text before moving it.

1 Position the cursor on the first character of the text you want to move.

2 Press Alt + F4 to select the **Block** command.

3 Press →, ←, ↓ or ↑ until you highlight all the text you want to move.

4 Press Alt + E to open the **Edit** menu.

5 Press E to select the **Cut and Paste** command.

SHORT CUT

Press Ctrl + Delete.

Move Text
Copy Text
Move/Copy Text Between Documents
Drag and Drop Text

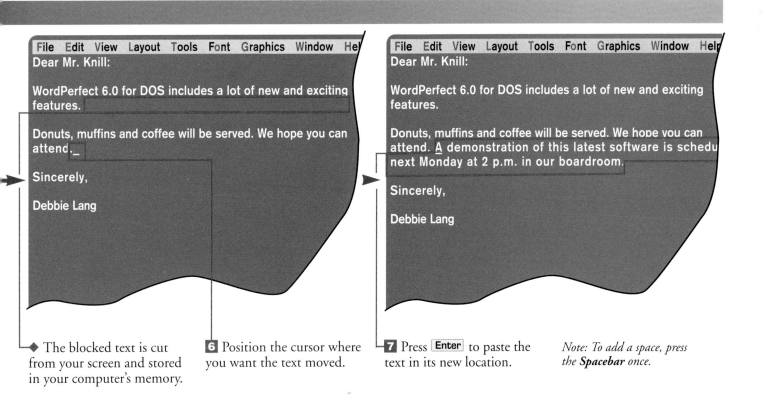

File Edit View Layout Tools Font Graphics Window Hel

Dear Mr. Knill:

WordPerfect 6.0 for DOS includes a lot of new and exciting features.

Donuts, muffins and coffee will be served. We hope you can attend._

Sincerely,

Debbie Lang

File Edit View Layout Tools Font Graphics Window Help

Dear Mr. Knill:

WordPerfect 6.0 for DOS includes a lot of new and exciting features.

Donuts, muffins and coffee will be served. We hope you can attend. A demonstration of this latest software is schedu next Monday at 2 p.m. in our boardroom.

Sincerely,

Debbie Lang

◆ The blocked text is cut from your screen and stored in your computer's memory.

6 Position the cursor where you want the text moved.

7 Press **Enter** to paste the text in its new location.

*Note: To add a space, press the **Spacebar** once.*

53

COPY
TEXT

You can copy text from one location in your document to another. WordPerfect "copies" the text and "pastes" it in a new location. The original text remains in its place.

Copy Text

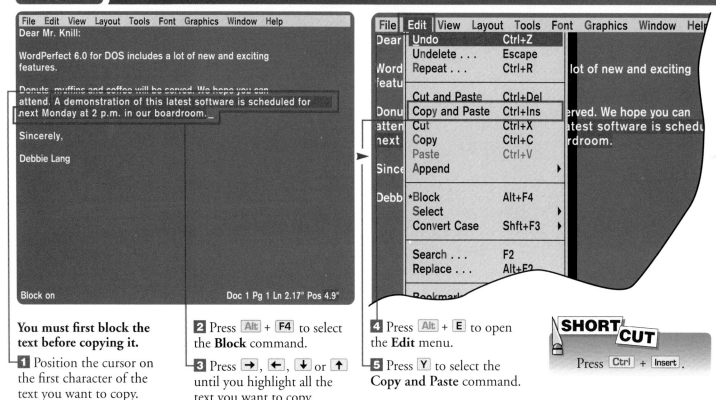

You must first block the text before copying it.

1 Position the cursor on the first character of the text you want to copy.

2 Press `Alt` + `F4` to select the **Block** command.

3 Press `→`, `←`, `↓` or `↑` until you highlight all the text you want to copy.

4 Press `Alt` + `E` to open the **Edit** menu.

5 Press `Y` to select the **Copy and Paste** command.

SHORT CUT

Press `Ctrl` + `Insert`.

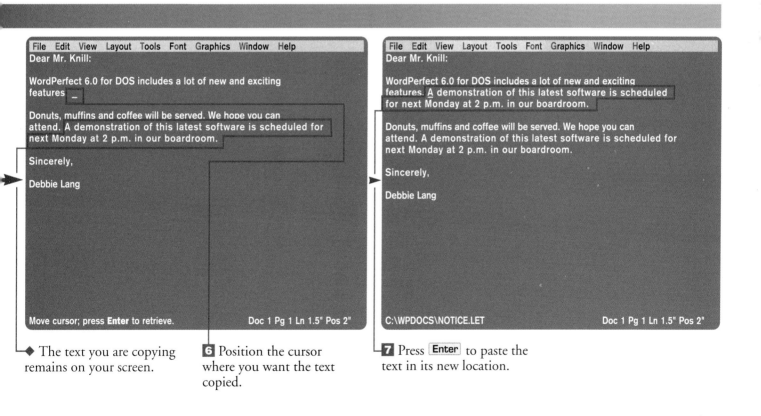

File Edit View Layout Tools Font Graphics Window Help

Dear Mr. Knill:

WordPerfect 6.0 for DOS includes a lot of new and exciting
features _

Donuts, muffins and coffee will be served. We hope you can
attend. A demonstration of this latest software is scheduled for
next Monday at 2 p.m. in our boardroom.

Sincerely,

Debbie Lang

Move cursor; press **Enter** to retrieve.   Doc 1 Pg 1 Ln 1.5" Pos 2"

File Edit View Layout Tools Font Graphics Window Help

Dear Mr. Knill:

WordPerfect 6.0 for DOS includes a lot of new and exciting
features. A demonstration of this latest software is scheduled
for next Monday at 2 p.m. in our boardroom.

Donuts, muffins and coffee will be served. We hope you can
attend. A demonstration of this latest software is scheduled for
next Monday at 2 p.m. in our boardroom.

Sincerely,

Debbie Lang

C:\WPDOCS\NOTICE.LET   Doc 1 Pg 1 Ln 1.5" Pos 2"

◆ The text you are copying
remains on your screen.

6 Position the cursor
where you want the text
copied.

7 Press **Enter** to paste the
text in its new location.

MOVE/COPY TEXT BETWEEN DOCUMENTS

Move or Copy Text Between Documents

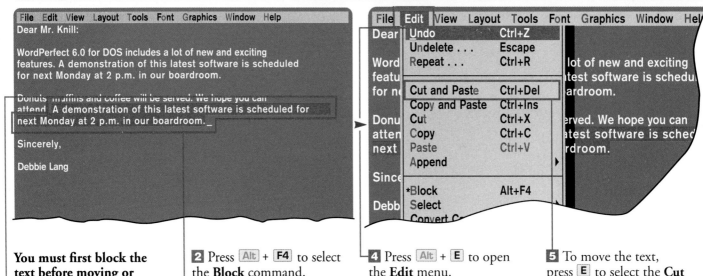

You must first block the text before moving or copying it.

1 Position the cursor on the first character of the text you want to move or copy.

2 Press `Alt` + `F4` to select the **Block** command.

3 Press `→`, `←`, `↓` or `↑` until you highlight all the text you want to move or copy.

4 Press `Alt` + `E` to open the Edit menu.

5 To move the text, press `E` to select the **Cut and Paste** command.

or

To copy the text, press `Y` to select the **Copy and Paste** command.

Getting
Started

Edit
Documents

Save and Open
Documents

Use Multiple
Documents

**Move and
Copy Text**

Check
Documents

Format
Documents

Change
Modes

Change
Fonts

Tables

Print
Documents

Merge
Documents

Move Text
Copy Text
Move/Copy Text Between Documents
Drag and Drop Text

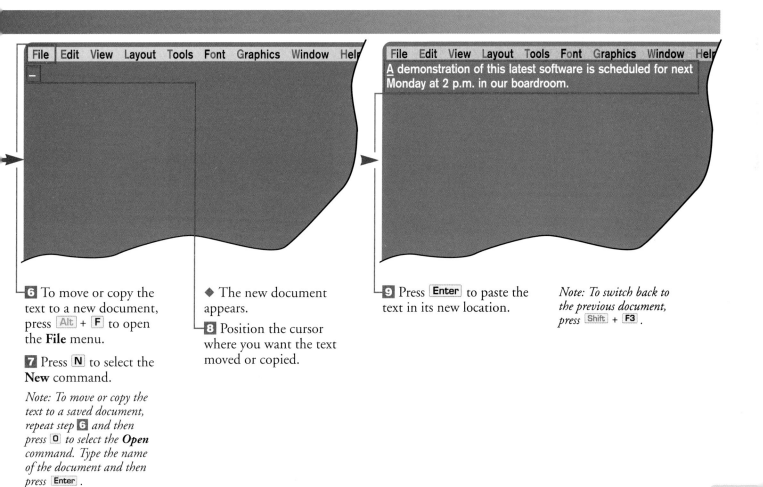

| File | Edit | View | Layout | Tools | Font | Graphics | Window | Help |

| File | Edit | View | Layout | Tools | Font | Graphics | Window | Help |

A demonstration of this latest software is scheduled for next Monday at 2 p.m. in our boardroom.

6 To move or copy the text to a new document, press Alt + F to open the **File** menu.

7 Press N to select the **New** command.

Note: To move or copy the text to a saved document, repeat step 6 and then press O to select the Open command. Type the name of the document and then press Enter.

◆ The new document appears.

8 Position the cursor where you want the text moved or copied.

9 Press Enter to paste the text in its new location.

Note: To switch back to the previous document, press Shift + F3.

DRAG AND DROP TEXT

You can move or copy text in your document by blocking the text and then dragging it to a new location.

The "drag and drop" feature only works with a mouse.

Drag and Drop Text

File	Edit	View	Layout	Tools	Font	Graphics	Window	Help

Dear Mr. Knill:

WordPerfect 6.0 for DOS includes a lot of new and exciting features. A demonstration of this latest software is schedul for next Monday at 2 p.m. in our boardroom.

Donuts, muffins and coffee will be served. We hope you can attend.

Sincerely,

Debbie Lang

File	Edit	View	Layout	Tools	Font	Graphics	Window	Help

Dear Mr. Knill:

WordPerfect 6.0 for DOS includes a lot of new and exciting features. A demonstration of this latest software is schedul for next Monday at 2 p.m. in our boardroom.

Donuts, muffins and coffee will be served. We hope you can attend.

Sincerely,

Debbie Lang

Move Text

1 Block the text you want to move.

*Note: To block a paragraph, position the mouse pointer anywhere in the paragraph. Then click the left mouse button **four times** in quick succession.*

For more information on blocking text, refer to page 14.

2 Position the mouse pointer on any character of the blocked text.

3 Press and hold down the left mouse button and then drag the pointer to where you want the text moved.

Move Text
Copy Text
Move/Copy Text Between Documents
Drag and Drop Text

UNDO CHANGES

The Undo command cancels your last editing action (example: drag and drop text). This only works immediately after you perform the action.

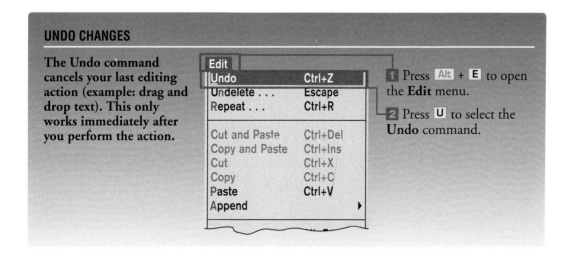

Edit	
Undo	Ctrl+Z
Undelete . . .	Escape
Repeat . . .	Ctrl+R
Cut and Paste	Ctrl+Del
Copy and Paste	Ctrl+Ins
Cut	Ctrl+X
Copy	Ctrl+C
Paste	Ctrl+V
Append	▶

1 Press Alt + E to open the **Edit** menu.

2 Press U to select the **Undo** command.

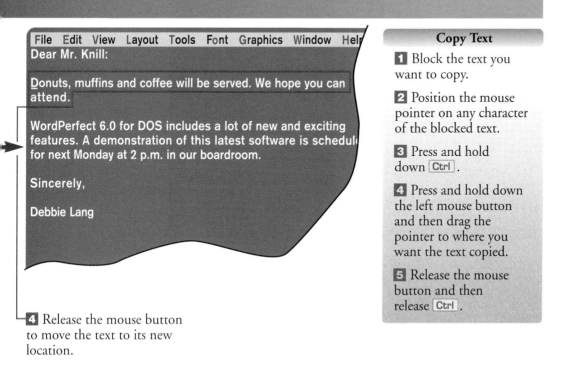

File Edit View Layout Tools Font Graphics Window Help

Dear Mr. Knill:

Donuts, muffins and coffee will be served. We hope you can attend.

WordPerfect 6.0 for DOS includes a lot of new and exciting features. A demonstration of this latest software is schedule for next Monday at 2 p.m. in our boardroom.

Sincerely,

Debbie Lang

4 Release the mouse button to move the text to its new location.

Copy Text

1 Block the text you want to copy.

2 Position the mouse pointer on any character of the blocked text.

3 Press and hold down Ctrl.

4 Press and hold down the left mouse button and then drag the pointer to where you want the text copied.

5 Release the mouse button and then release Ctrl.

SEARCH FOR TEXT

The Search feature helps you find a word or phrase in your document.

Search for Text

File Edit View Layout Tools Font Graphics Window Hel

Dear Mr. Knill:

WordPerfect 6.0 for DOS includes a lot of new and exciting features. A demonstration of this latest software is sched for next Monday at 2 p.m. in our boardroom.

Donuts, muffins and coffee will be served. We hope you can attend.

Sincerely,

Debbie Lang

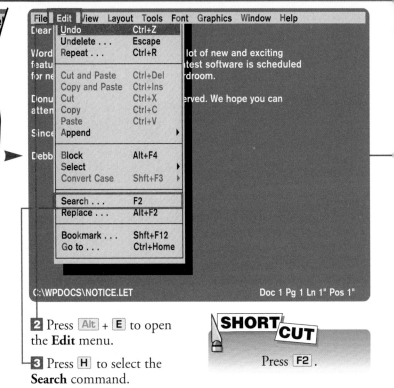

File	Edit	View Layout Tools Font Graphics Window Help
Dear	Undo	Ctrl+Z
	Undelete . . .	Escape
Word	Repeat . . .	Ctrl+R
featu		
for ne	Cut and Paste	Ctrl+Del
	Copy and Paste	Ctrl+Ins
Donu	Cut	Ctrl+X
atten	Copy	Ctrl+C
	Paste	Ctrl+V
Since	Append	▶
Debb	Block	Alt+F4
	Select	▶
	Convert Case	Shft+F3 ▶
	Search . . .	F2
	Replace . . .	Alt+F2
	Bookmark . . .	Shft+F12
	Go to . . .	Ctrl+Home

lot of new and exciting
atest software is scheduled
rdroom.

erved. We hope you can

C:\WPDOCS\NOTICE.LET   Doc 1 Pg 1 Ln 1" Pos 1"

1 Position the cursor where you want the search to begin.

2 Press Alt + E to open the **Edit** menu.

3 Press H to select the **Search** command.

SHORT CUT

Press F2.

| Getting Started | Edit Documents | Save and Open Documents | Use Multiple Documents | Move and Copy Text | **Check Documents** | Format Documents | Change Modes | Change Fonts | Tables | Print Documents | Merge Documents |

Search for Text
Replace Text
Speller
Thesaurus

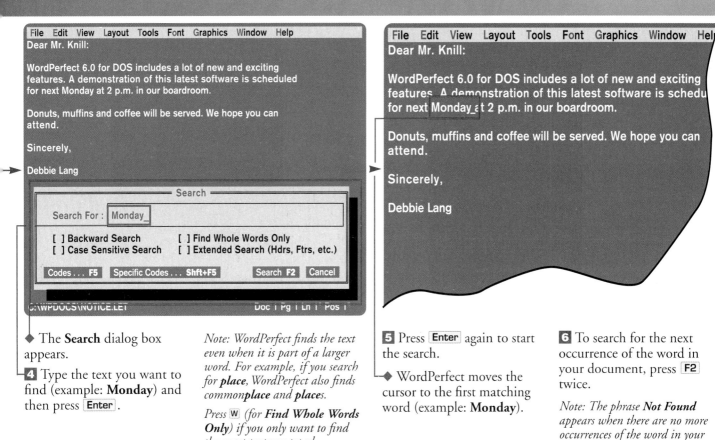

File Edit View Layout Tools Font Graphics Window Help

Dear Mr. Knill:

WordPerfect 6.0 for DOS includes a lot of new and exciting features. A demonstration of this latest software is scheduled for next Monday at 2 p.m. in our boardroom.

Donuts, muffins and coffee will be served. We hope you can attend.

Sincerely,

Debbie Lang

```
┌──────────────────────── Search ────────────────────────┐
│                                                         │
│  Search For :  Monday_                                  │
│                                                         │
│  [ ] Backward Search        [ ] Find Whole Words Only   │
│  [ ] Case Sensitive Search  [ ] Extended Search (Hdrs, Ftrs, etc.) │
│  Codes... F5   Specific Codes... Shft+F5   Search F2  Cancel │
└─────────────────────────────────────────────────────────┘
```

C:\WPDOCS\NOTICE.LET   Doc 1 Pg 1 Ln 1 Pos 1

File Edit View Layout Tools Font Graphics Window Hel

Dear Mr. Knill:

WordPerfect 6.0 for DOS includes a lot of new and exciting features. A demonstration of this latest software is schedu for next Monday at 2 p.m. in our boardroom.

Donuts, muffins and coffee will be served. We hope you can attend.

Sincerely,

Debbie Lang

◆ The **Search** dialog box appears.

4 Type the text you want to find (example: **Monday**) and then press `Enter`.

*Note: WordPerfect finds the text even when it is part of a larger word. For example, if you search for **place**, WordPerfect also finds common**place** and **place**s.*

*Press `W` (for **Find Whole Words Only**) if you only want to find the exact text you typed.*

5 Press `Enter` again to start the search.

◆ WordPerfect moves the cursor to the first matching word (example: **Monday**).

6 To search for the next occurrence of the word in your document, press `F2` twice.

*Note: The phrase **Not Found** appears when there are no more occurrences of the word in your document. Press `Enter` to return to your document.*

Replace Text

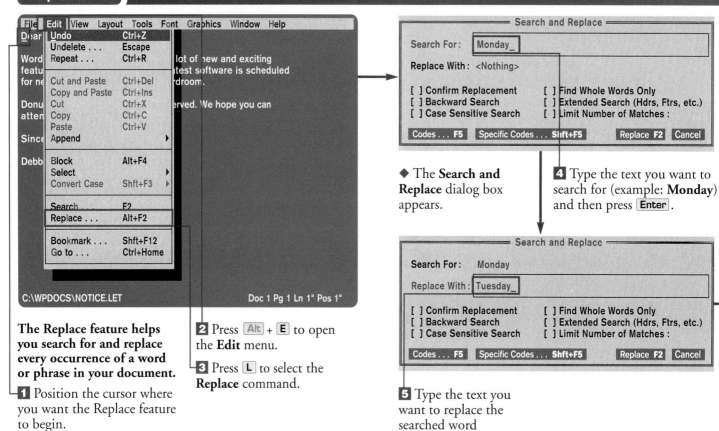

◆ The **Search and Replace** dialog box appears.

4 Type the text you want to search for (example: **Monday**) and then press **Enter**.

The Replace feature helps you search for and replace every occurrence of a word or phrase in your document.

1 Position the cursor where you want the Replace feature to begin.

2 Press **Alt** + **E** to open the **Edit** menu.

3 Press **L** to select the **Replace** command.

5 Type the text you want to replace the searched word (example: **Tuesday**) and then press **Enter**.

TIP

◆ The Replace feature is ideal when you have frequently misspelled a word in your document.

| Getting Started | Edit Documents | Save and Open Documents | Use Multiple Documents | Move and Copy Text | **Check Documents** | Format Documents | Change Modes | Change Fonts | Tables | Print Documents | Merge Documents |

Search for Text
Replace Text
Speller
Thesaurus

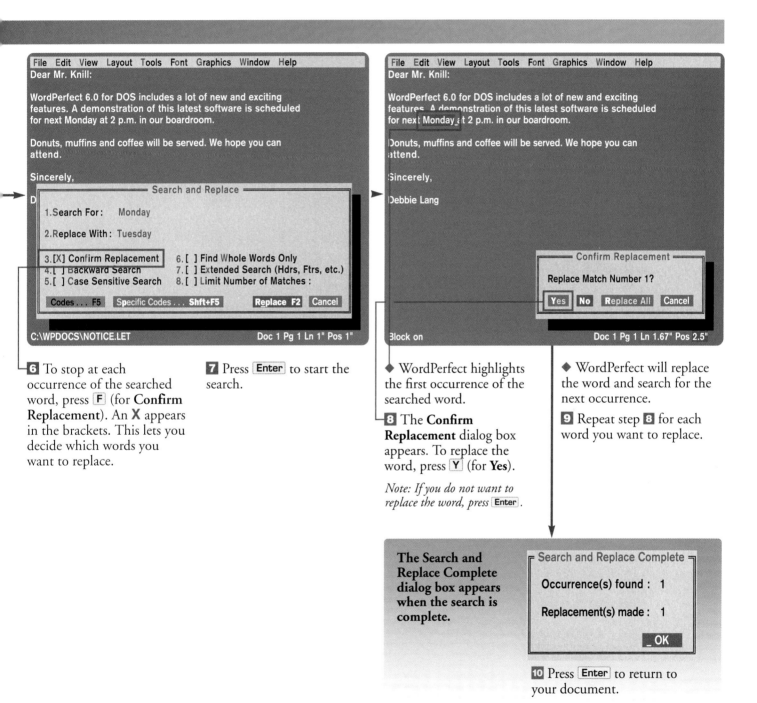

6 To stop at each occurrence of the searched word, press **F** (for **Confirm Replacement**). An **X** appears in the brackets. This lets you decide which words you want to replace.

7 Press **Enter** to start the search.

◆ WordPerfect highlights the first occurrence of the searched word.

8 The **Confirm Replacement** dialog box appears. To replace the word, press **Y** (for **Yes**).

Note: If you do not want to replace the word, press Enter.

◆ WordPerfect will replace the word and search for the next occurrence.

9 Repeat step **8** for each word you want to replace.

The Search and Replace Complete dialog box appears when the search is complete.

10 Press **Enter** to return to your document.

The Speller checks your document for spelling errors.

Every word in your document is compared to WordPerfect's own dictionary. If WordPerfect cannot match a word, it is considered misspelled.

Spell Check Your Document

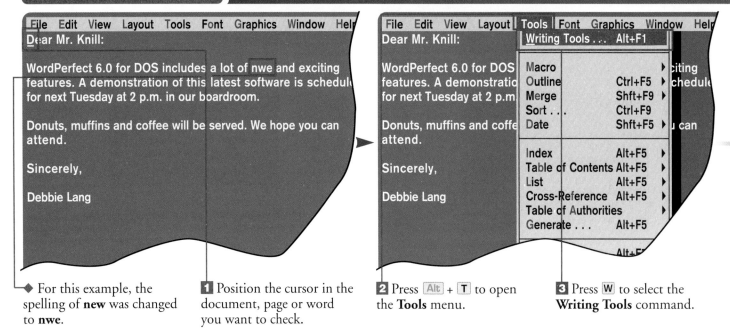

◆ For this example, the spelling of **new** was changed to **nwe**.

1 Position the cursor in the document, page or word you want to check.

2 Press Alt + T to open the **Tools** menu.

3 Press W to select the **Writing Tools** command.

THE SPELLER FINDS:

◆ Misspelled words
(example: The girl is six **yearss** old).

◆ Duplicate words
(example: The girl is **six six** years old).

◆ Capitalization errors
(example: **TH**e girl is six years old).

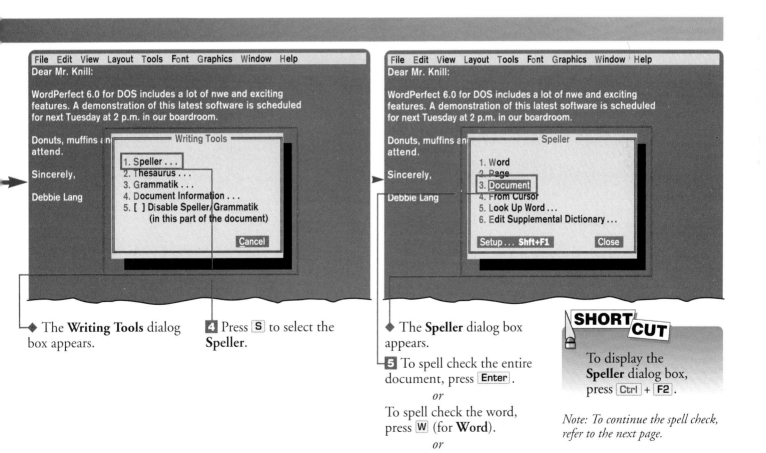

File Edit View Layout Tools Font Graphics Window Help
Dear Mr. Knill:

WordPerfect 6.0 for DOS includes a lot of nwe and exciting features. A demonstration of this latest software is scheduled for next Tuesday at 2 p.m. in our boardroom.

Donuts, muffins an
attend.

Sincerely,

Debbie Lang

── Writing Tools ──
1. Speller . . .
2. Thesaurus . . .
3. Grammatik . . .
4. Document Information . . .
5. [ ] Disable Speller/Grammatik
    (in this part of the document)

Cancel

File Edit View Layout Tools Font Graphics Window Help
Dear Mr. Knill:

WordPerfect 6.0 for DOS includes a lot of nwe and exciting features. A demonstration of this latest software is scheduled for next Tuesday at 2 p.m. in our boardroom.

Donuts, muffins an
attend.

Sincerely,

Debbie Lang

── Speller ──
1. Word
2. Page
3. Document
4. From Cursor
5. Look Up Word . . .
6. Edit Supplemental Dictionary . . .

Setup . . . **Shft+F1**   Close

◆ The **Writing Tools** dialog box appears.

4 Press **S** to select the **Speller**.

◆ The **Speller** dialog box appears.

5 To spell check the entire document, press **Enter**.
or
To spell check the word, press **W** (for **Word**).
or
To spell check the page, press **P** (for **Page**).

SHORT CUT

To display the **Speller** dialog box, press **Ctrl** + **F2**.

Note: To continue the spell check, refer to the next page.

Spell Check Your Document (Continued)

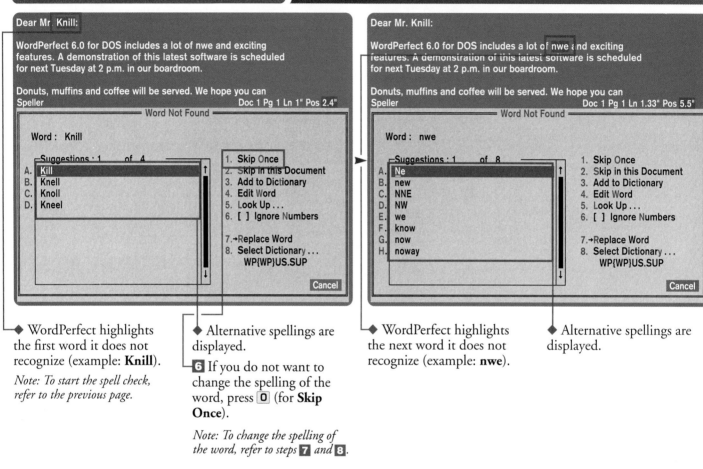

◆ WordPerfect highlights the first word it does not recognize (example: **Knill**).

Note: To start the spell check, refer to the previous page.

◆ Alternative spellings are displayed.

6 If you do not want to change the spelling of the word, press **O** (for **Skip Once**).

*Note: To change the spelling of the word, refer to steps **7** and **8**.*

◆ WordPerfect highlights the next word it does not recognize (example: **nwe**).

◆ Alternative spellings are displayed.

SPELL CHECK OPTIONS

Skip Once	Press **O** to keep the current spelling of the word in this instance only.	**Edit Word**	Press **W** to manually change the word in your document. Press **Enter** to return to the spell check.
Skip in this Document	Press **S** to keep the current spelling of the word and skip every occurrence in the document.	**Look Up**	Press **L** to check the spelling of a different word. Type the word and then press **Enter**. Press **Esc** twice to return to the spell check.
Add to Dictionary	Press **T** to permanently add the word to the WordPerfect dictionary. The speller then considers it correctly spelled for all future documents.	**[ ] Ignore Numbers**	Press **N** to skip words that contain both letters and numbers. An **X** appears in the brackets when you select this option.

Search for Text
Replace Text
Speller
Thesaurus

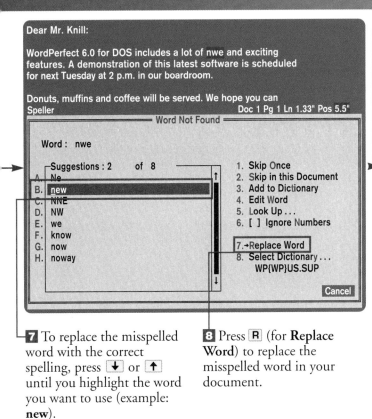

Dear Mr. Knill:

WordPerfect 6.0 for DOS includes a lot of nwe and exciting features. A demonstration of this latest software is scheduled for next Tuesday at 2 p.m. in our boardroom.

Donuts, muffins and coffee will be served. We hope you can
Speller   Doc 1 Pg 1 Ln 1.33" Pos 5.5"

─ Word Not Found ─

Word : nwe

Suggestions : 2   of 8
A. Ne
B. new
C. NNE
D. NW
E. we
F. know
G. now
H. noway

1. Skip Once
2. Skip in this Document
3. Add to Dictionary
4. Edit Word
5. Look Up . . .
6. [ ] Ignore Numbers
7.→Replace Word
8. Select Dictionary . . .
   WP{WP}US.SUP

Cancel

WordPerfect 6.0 for DOS includes a lot of new and exciting features. A demonstration of this latest software is scheduled for next Tuesday at 2 p.m. in our boardroom.

Donuts, muffins and coffee will be served. We hope you can attend.
Speller   Doc 1 Pg 1 Ln 1.67" Pos 4.4"

Spell Check Completed.

_OK

7 To replace the misspelled word with the correct spelling, press ↓ or ↑ until you highlight the word you want to use (example: **new**).

8 Press **R** (for **Replace Word**) to replace the misspelled word in your document.

◆ WordPerfect corrects the word and continues checking your document.

9 Repeat step **6** (or steps **7** and **8**) until WordPerfect finishes checking your document.

◆ This dialog box appears when the spell check is complete.

10 Press **Enter** to exit the speller and return to your document.

To cancel the spell check at any time, press Esc.

The WordPerfect Thesaurus helps you add variety to your writing. You can look up a word from your document and replace it with a different one.

TACKLE
- Attempt
- Endeavor

WP Thesaurus
New 6.0 Edition

Using the Thesaurus

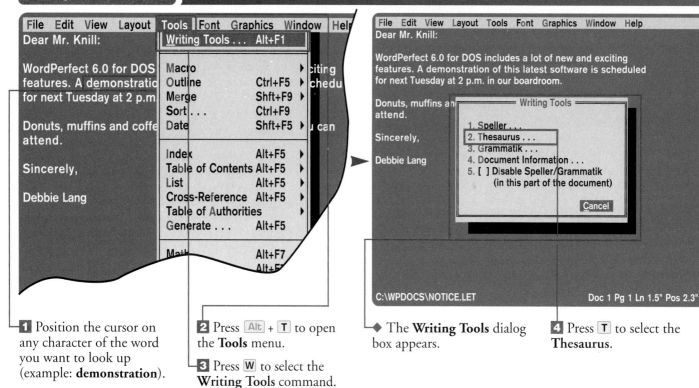

File Edit View Layout **Tools** Font Graphics Window Hel

Dear Mr. Knill:

Writing Tools . . . Alt+F1

WordPerfect 6.0 for DOS
features. A demonstratio
for next Tuesday at 2 p.m.

Macro
Outline   Ctrl+F5
Merge   Shft+F9
Sort . . .   Ctrl+F9
Date   Shft+F5

citing
chedu

Donuts, muffins and coffe
attend.

u can

Sincerely,

Index   Alt+F5
Table of Contents   Alt+F5
List   Alt+F5
Cross-Reference   Alt+F5
Table of Authorities
Generate . . .   Alt+F5

Debbie Lang

Math   Alt+F7
                     Alt+F

File Edit View Layout Tools Font Graphics Window Help

Dear Mr. Knill:

WordPerfect 6.0 for DOS includes a lot of new and exciting features. A demonstration of this latest software is scheduled for next Tuesday at 2 p.m. in our boardroom.

Donuts, muffins an
attend.

Sincerely,

Debbie Lang

Writing Tools

1. Speller . . .
2. Thesaurus . . .
3. Grammatik . . .
4. Document Information . . .
5. [ ] Disable Speller/Grammatik
       (in this part of the document)

Cancel

C:\WPDOCS\NOTICE.LET   Doc 1 Pg 1 Ln 1.5" Pos 2.3"

1 Position the cursor on any character of the word you want to look up (example: **demonstration**).

2 Press Alt + T to open the **Tools** menu.

3 Press W to select the **Writing Tools** command.

◆ The **Writing Tools** dialog box appears.

4 Press T to select the **Thesaurus**.

Search for Text
Replace Text
Speller
Thesaurus

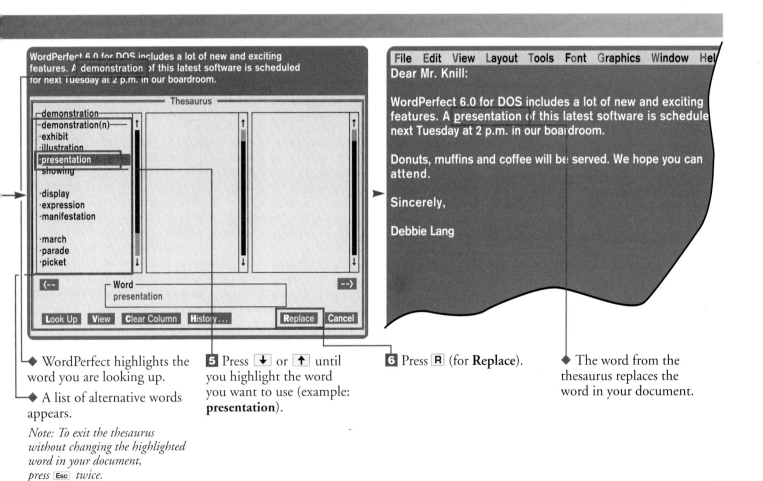

◆ WordPerfect highlights the word you are looking up.

◆ A list of alternative words appears.

Note: To exit the thesaurus without changing the highlighted word in your document, press Esc *twice.*

5 Press ↓ or ↑ until you highlight the word you want to use (example: **presentation**).

6 Press **R** (for **Replace**).

◆ The word from the thesaurus replaces the word in your document.

JUSTIFY TEXT

There are different ways you can align text in your document.

◆ **Center** justification

◆ **Right** justification

◆ **Left** justification

◆ **Full** justification

Justify Text

File   Edit   View   Layout   Tools   Font   Graphics   Window   Hel

Dear Mr. Knill:

WordPerfect 6.0 for DOS includes a lot of new and exciting features. A presentation of this latest software is schedule next Tuesday at 2 p.m. in our boardroom.

Donuts, muffins and coffee will be served. We hope you can attend.

Sincerely,

Debbie Lang

1 Position the cursor where you want the new justification to begin.

CENTER ONE LINE OF TEXT

1 To center one line of text, position the cursor on the first character of the text.

2 Press `Alt` + `L` to open the **Layout** menu.

3 Press `A` to select the **Alignment** command.

4 Press `C` (for **Center**).

Note: To right align one line of text, press `F` (for Flush Right).

SHORT CUT

To center the current line of text, press `Shift` + `F6`.

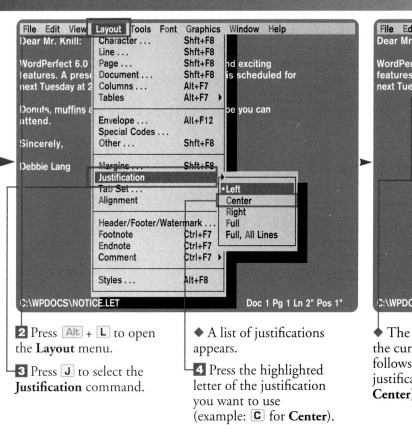

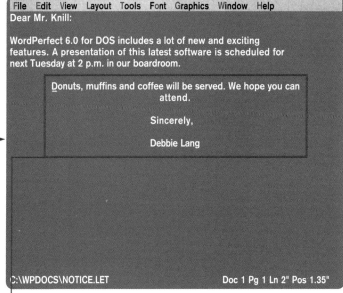

2 Press `Alt` + `L` to open the **Layout** menu.

3 Press `J` to select the **Justification** command.

◆ A list of justifications appears.

4 Press the highlighted letter of the justification you want to use (example: `C` for **Center**).

◆ The paragraph containing the cursor and all text that follows display the new justification (example: **Center**).

Note: WordPerfect cannot display fully justified text on your screen. To view this format, refer to "Preview a Document" on page 112.

DELETE A FORMATTING CODE

To remove a format from your document, you can delete its code.

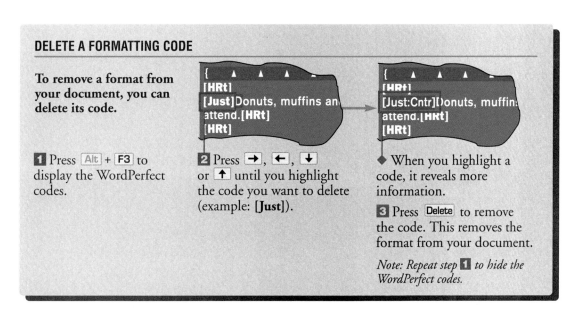

1 Press `Alt` + `F3` to display the WordPerfect codes.

2 Press `→`, `←`, `↓` or `↑` until you highlight the code you want to delete (example: **[Just]**).

◆ When you highlight a code, it reveals more information.

3 Press `Delete` to remove the code. This removes the format from your document.

*Note: Repeat step **1** to hide the WordPerfect codes.*

CHANGE MARGINS

A margin is the amount of space between the text and the edges of your paper.

You can shorten or lengthen the size of your document by changing the margins.

FORMAT

◆ 2 inch margin   ◆ 1 inch margin

The World Report

Change Margins

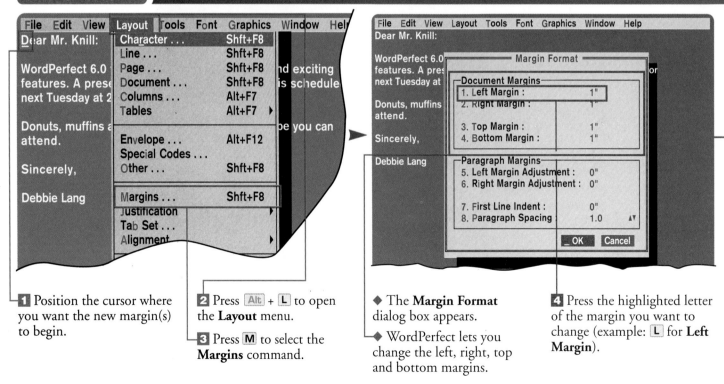

1 Position the cursor where you want the new margin(s) to begin.

2 Press Alt + L to open the **Layout** menu.

3 Press M to select the **Margins** command.

◆ The **Margin Format** dialog box appears.

◆ WordPerfect lets you change the left, right, top and bottom margins.

4 Press the highlighted letter of the margin you want to change (example: L for **Left Margin**).

When you create a document, WordPerfect automatically sets a one-inch margin on the Left, Right, Top and Bottom edges of your page. However, you can change these settings.

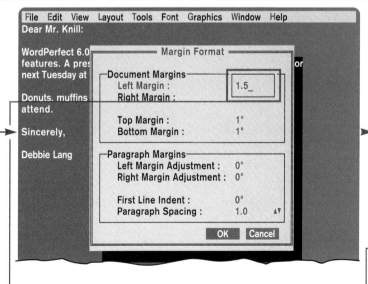

5 Type a new margin in inches (example: **1.5**) and then press **Enter**.

*Note: Repeat steps **4** and **5** for each margin you want to change.*

6 Press **Enter** again to return to your document.

◆ The paragraph containing the cursor and all text that follows display the new margin(s).

Note: WordPerfect cannot display top and bottom margins on your screen. To view them, refer to "Preview a Document" on page 112.

CHANGE
LINE SPACING

You can change the amount of space between the lines of text in your document.

When you type text, WordPerfect automatically single spaces the text.

◆ **Single spacing**   ◆ **Double spacing**

Change Line Spacing

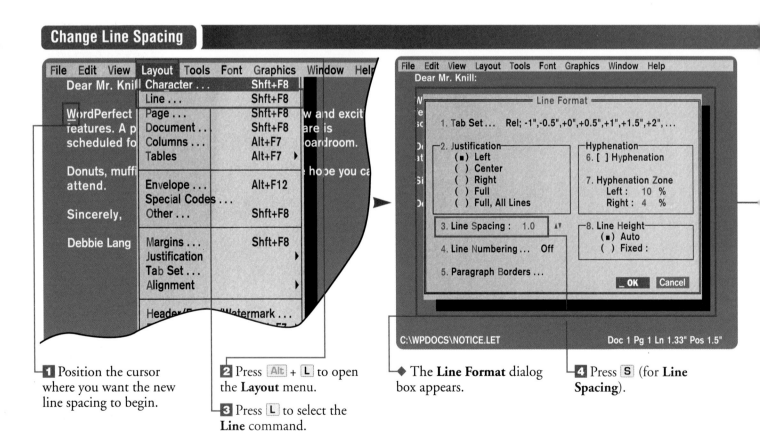

1 Position the cursor where you want the new line spacing to begin.

2 Press `Alt` + `L` to open the **Layout** menu.

3 Press `L` to select the **Line** command.

◆ The **Line Format** dialog box appears.

4 Press `S` (for **Line Spacing**).

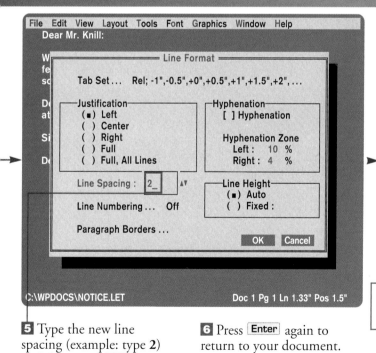

File Edit View Layout Tools Font Graphics Window Help
Dear Mr. Knill:

┌─────────────────────── Line Format ───────────────────────┐

  Tab Set ...   Rel; -1",-0.5",+0",+0.5",+1",+1.5",+2", ...

  ┌─Justification─────────┐   ┌─Hyphenation─────────┐
  │ (■) Left   │   │ [ ] Hyphenation   │
  │ ( ) Center   │   │   │
  │ ( ) Right   │   │ Hyphenation Zone   │
  │ ( ) Full   │   │   Left :   10 %   │
  │ ( ) Full, All Lines   │   │   Right :   4 %   │
  └───────────────────────┘   └─────────────────────┘

  Line Spacing : [2_] ▲▼   ┌─Line Height─────────┐
                              │ (■) Auto   │
  Line Numbering ... Off   │ ( ) Fixed :   │
                              └─────────────────────┘
  Paragraph Borders ...
                                        [OK] [Cancel]
└───┘

C:\WPDOCS\NOTICE.LET   Doc 1 Pg 1 Ln 1.33" Pos 1.5"

File Edit View Layout Tools Font Graphics Window Help
Dear Mr. Knill:

WordPerfect 6.0 for DOS includes a lot of new and exciting

features. A presentation of this latest software is

scheduled for next Tuesday at 2 p.m. in our boardroom.

Donuts, muffins and coffee will be served. We hope you can

attend.

Sincerely,

Debbie Lang

C:\WPDOCS\NOTICE.LET   Doc 1 Pg 1 Ln 1.33" Pos 1.5"

5 Type the new line spacing (example: type **2**) and then press `Enter`.

6 Press `Enter` again to return to your document.

◆ The paragraph containing the cursor and all text that follows display the new line spacing (example: **double spacing**).

*Note: To return to single spacing, delete the line spacing code ([**Ln Spacing**]). For information on deleting a formatting code, refer to page 71.*

CHANGE TAB SETTINGS

You can use tabs to line up columns of information or to indent a line of text.

WORDPERFECT OFFERS FOUR TYPES OF TABS:

Left Tab	Center Tab	Right Tab	Decimal Tab
Jim	Devries	June 1993	$50.00
David	Johnston	July 1993	$110.00
Richard	Morton	August 1993	$9.00
Betty	Wong	September 1993	$65.00

Delete a Tab

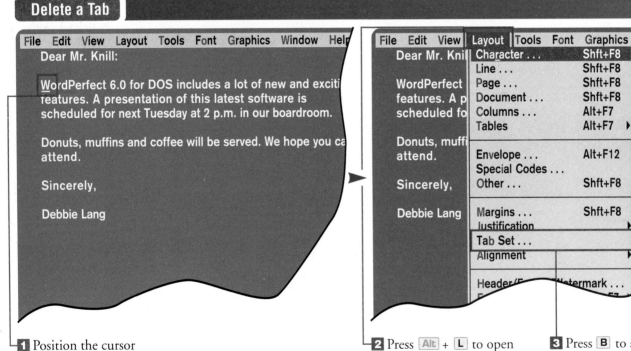

1 Position the cursor where you want the new tab settings to begin.

2 Press `Alt` + `L` to open the **Layout** menu.

3 Press `B` to select the **Tab Set** command.

Justify Text
Change Margins
Change Line Spacing
Change Tab Settings
Indent Text

Center a Page
Add Page Numbers
Add Headers or Footers
Change Paper Size and Type

To insert a row of dots before a tab, you can make it a dot leader tab. Dot leaders "lead" the eye from one column of information to another. You can use them when creating a Table of Contents.

Jim.................Devries ....June 1993 ....$50.00
David...........Johnston ....July 1993 ....$110.00
Richard..........Morton ....August 1993 ....$9.
Betty ....Wong ....September 1993 ....$65.

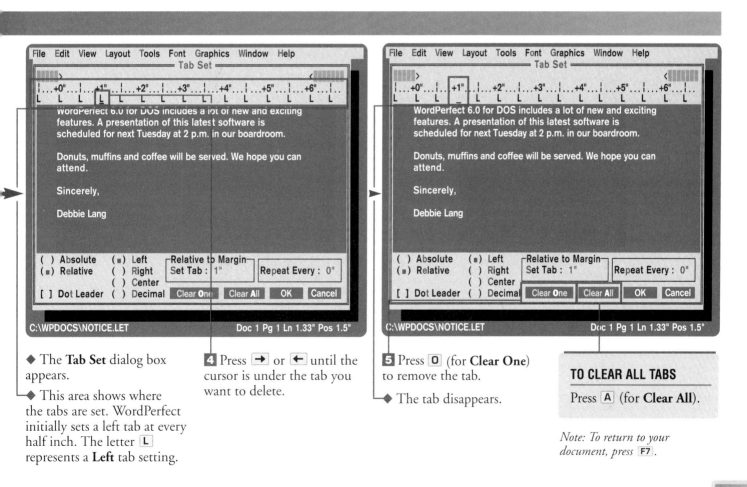

◆ The **Tab Set** dialog box appears.

◆ This area shows where the tabs are set. WordPerfect initially sets a left tab at every half inch. The letter **L** represents a **Left** tab setting.

4 Press **→** or **←** until the cursor is under the tab you want to delete.

5 Press **O** (for **Clear One**) to remove the tab.

◆ The tab disappears.

TO CLEAR ALL TABS

Press **A** (for **Clear All**).

*Note: To return to your document, press **F7**.*

CHANGE TAB SETTINGS

You can add a tab to help you line up text in your document.

L for
Left
Tab

C for
Center
Tab

R for
Right
Tab

D for
Decimal
Tab

Add a Tab

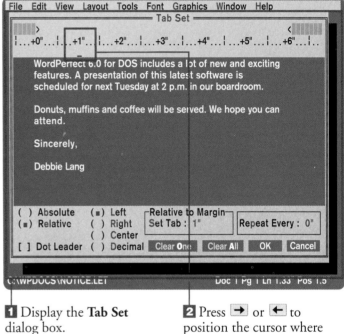

1 Display the **Tab Set** dialog box.

*Note: To display the **Tab Set** dialog box, refer to page 76.*

2 Press → or ← to position the cursor where you want to add a tab.

Using Tabs

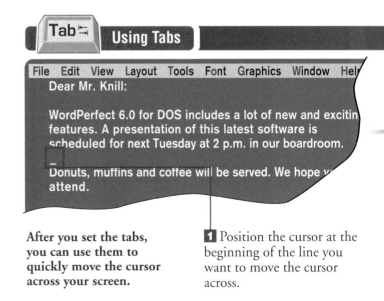

After you set the tabs, you can use them to quickly move the cursor across your screen.

1 Position the cursor at the beginning of the line you want to move the cursor across.

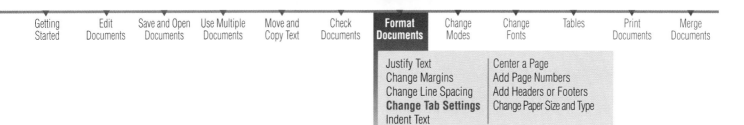

Justify Text   Center a Page
Change Margins   Add Page Numbers
Change Line Spacing   Add Headers or Footers
Change Tab Settings   Change Paper Size and Type
Indent Text

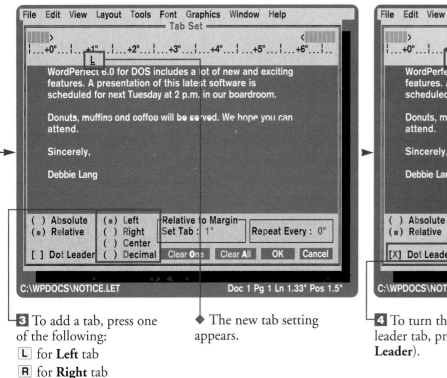

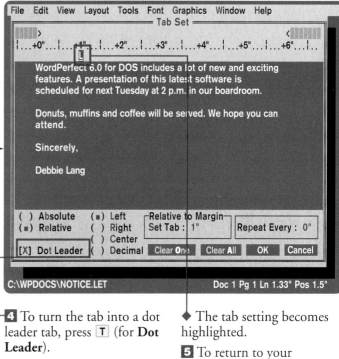

3 To add a tab, press one of the following:

⌨ **L** for **Left** tab
⌨ **R** for **Right** tab
⌨ **C** for **Center** tab
⌨ **D** for **Decimal** tab

◆ The new tab setting appears.

4 To turn the tab into a dot leader tab, press **T** (for **Dot Leader**).

◆ The tab setting becomes highlighted.

5 To return to your document, press **F7**.

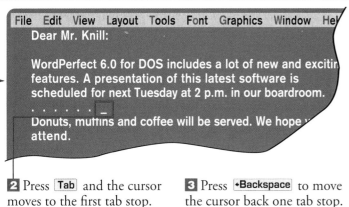

2 Press **Tab** and the cursor moves to the first tab stop.

Note: If you have more than one tab setting, press Tab again to move to the next tab stop.

3 Press **◄Backspace** to move the cursor back one tab stop.

INDENT
TEXT

Indent

To emphasize a paragraph in your document, WordPerfect offers different ways to indent it.

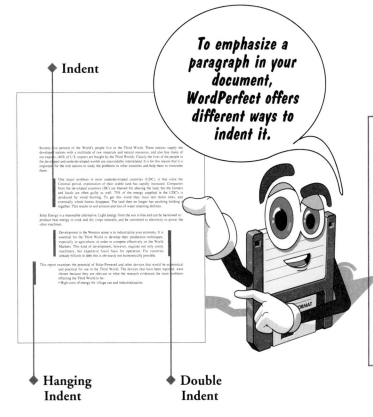

Hanging Indent

Double Indent

File Edit View Layout Tools Font Graphics Window Hel

Dear Mr. Knill:

WordPerfect 6.0 for DOS includes a lot of new and excit features. A presentation of this latest software is scheduled for next Tuesday at 2 p.m. in our boardroom.

Donuts, muffins and coffee will be served. We hope you ca attend.

Sincerely,

Debbie Lang

1 Position the cursor on the first character of the paragraph you want to indent.

INDENT NEW TEXT

1 Position the cursor at the beginning of the line where you want the new text to appear.

2 Press Alt + L to open the **Layout** menu.

3 Press A to select the **Alignment** command.

4 Press the highlighted letter of the style of indent you want to use.

5 Type the text.

6 Press Enter to turn off the indent.

Justify Text
Change Margins
Change Line Spacing
Change Tab Settings
Indent Text

Center a Page
Add Page Numbers
Add Headers or Footers
Change Paper Size and Type

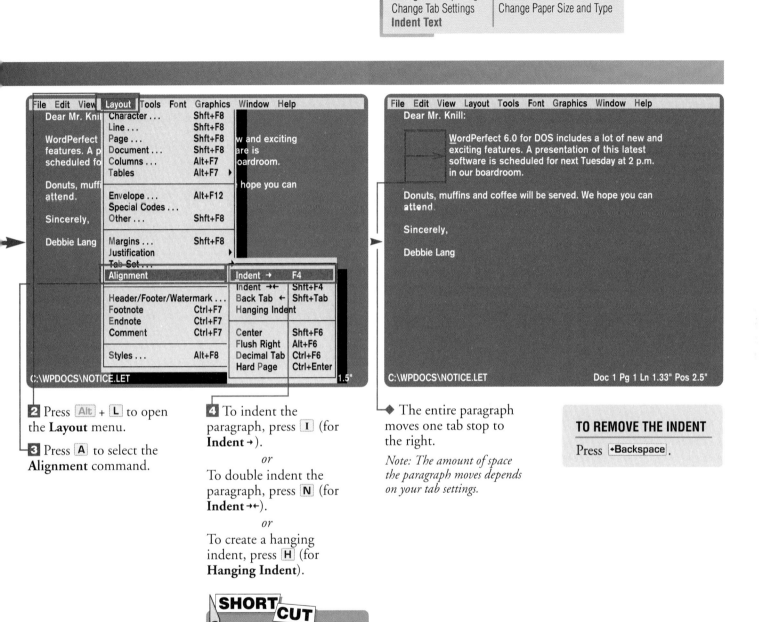

2 Press `Alt` + `L` to open the **Layout** menu.

3 Press `A` to select the **Alignment** command.

4 To indent the paragraph, press `I` (for **Indent →**).

or

To double indent the paragraph, press `N` (for **Indent →←**).

or

To create a hanging indent, press `H` (for **Hanging Indent**).

◆ The entire paragraph moves one tab stop to the right.

Note: The amount of space the paragraph moves depends on your tab settings.

TO REMOVE THE INDENT

Press `←Backspace`.

SHORT CUT

for steps 2 to 4

◆ To indent the paragraph, press `F4`.

◆ To double indent the paragraph, press `Shift` + `F4`.

CENTER A PAGE

WordPerfect lets you vertically center text on your page. This is useful when creating title pages or short memos.

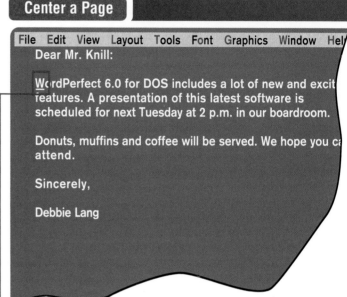

Center a Page

File Edit View Layout Tools Font Graphics Window Hel

Dear Mr. Knill:

WordPerfect 6.0 for DOS includes a lot of new and excit features. A presentation of this latest software is scheduled for next Tuesday at 2 p.m. in our boardroom.

Donuts, muffins and coffee will be served. We hope you c attend.

Sincerely,

Debbie Lang

1 Position the cursor anywhere on the page you want to center vertically.

START A NEW PAGE

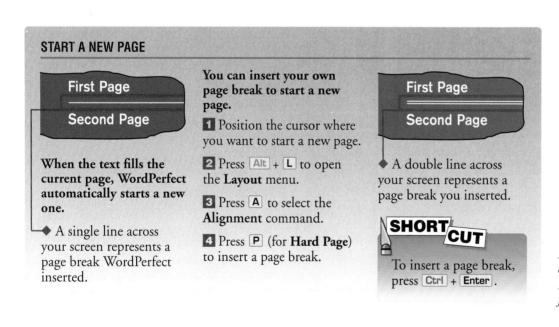

When the text fills the current page, WordPerfect automatically starts a new one.

◆ A single line across your screen represents a page break WordPerfect inserted.

You can insert your own page break to start a new page.

1 Position the cursor where you want to start a new page.

2 Press `Alt` + `L` to open the **Layout** menu.

3 Press `A` to select the **Alignment** command.

4 Press `P` (for **Hard Page**) to insert a page break.

◆ A double line across your screen represents a page break you inserted.

SHORT CUT

To insert a page break, press `Ctrl` + `Enter`.

*Note: To remove a page break, delete its code ([**HPg**]).*

For information on deleting a formatting code, refer to page 71.

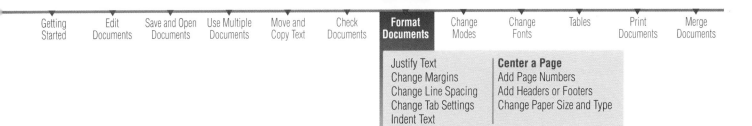

Justify Text
Change Margins
Change Line Spacing
Change Tab Settings
Indent Text

Center a Page
Add Page Numbers
Add Headers or Footers
Change Paper Size and Type

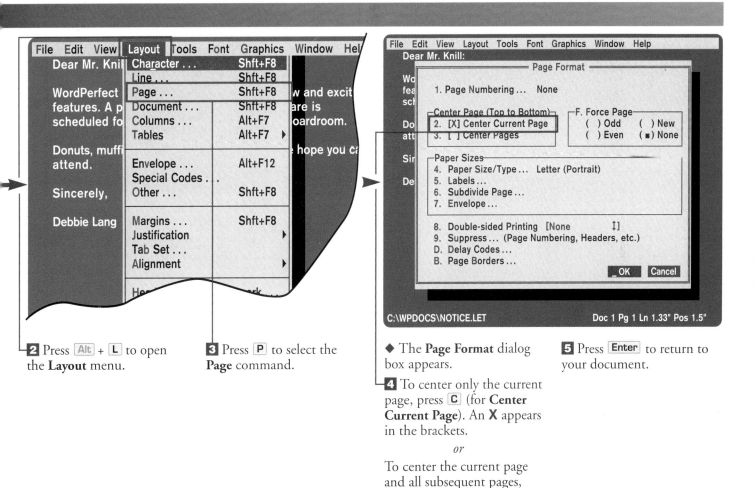

2 Press `Alt` + `L` to open the **Layout** menu.

3 Press `P` to select the **Page** command.

◆ The **Page Format** dialog box appears.

4 To center only the current page, press `C` (for **Center Current Page**). An **X** appears in the brackets.

or

To center the current page and all subsequent pages, press `P` (for **Center Pages**). An **X** appears in the brackets.

5 Press `Enter` to return to your document.

◆ Your screen does not display the text vertically centered, but this format will appear **TIP** when you print your document.

Note: To view your page vertically centered, refer to "Preview a Document" on page 112.

ADD PAGE NUMBERS

WordPerfect can automatically number the pages in your document.

Add Page Numbers

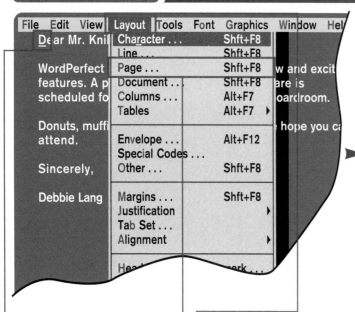

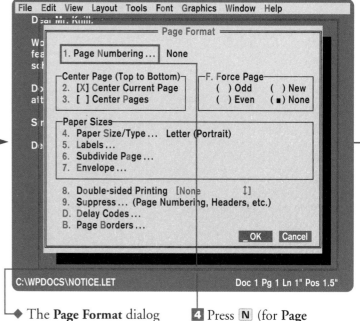

1 Position the cursor anywhere on the page where you want the numbering to begin.

2 Press `Alt` + `L` to open the **Layout** menu.

3 Press `P` to select the **Page** command.

◆ The **Page Format** dialog box appears.

4 Press `N` (for **Page Numbering**).

Getting
Started

Edit
Documents

Save and Open
Documents

Use Multiple
Documents

Move and
Copy Text

Check
Documents

**Format
Documents**

Change
Modes

Change
Fonts

Tables

Print
Documents

Merge
Documents

Justify Text
Change Margins
Change Line Spacing
Change Tab Settings
Indent Text

Center a Page
Add Page Numbers
Add Headers or Footers
Change Paper Size and Type

TIP ◆ Your screen does not
display the page numbers,
but they will appear when
you print your document.

*Note: To view the page numbers
in your document, refer to
"Preview a Document" on
page 112.*

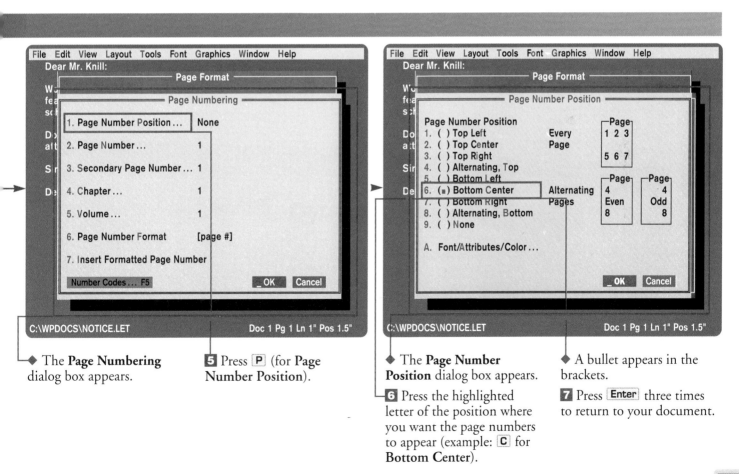

◆ The **Page Numbering**
dialog box appears.

5 Press **P** (for **Page
Number Position**).

◆ The **Page Number
Position** dialog box appears.

6 Press the highlighted
letter of the position where
you want the page numbers
to appear (example: **C** for
Bottom Center).

◆ A bullet appears in the
brackets.

7 Press **Enter** three times
to return to your document.

ADD HEADERS OR FOOTERS

> *A Header is information you place at the top of a page. A Footer is information you place at the bottom of a page. Headers and Footers may include a company name, a date or the title of your document. They can appear on every page or on alternate pages.*

◆ Header

◆ Footer

Add Headers or Footers

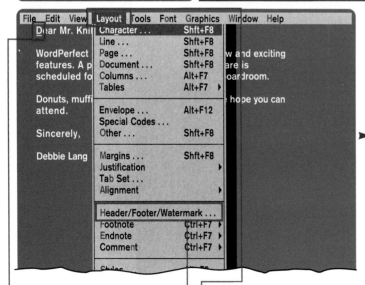

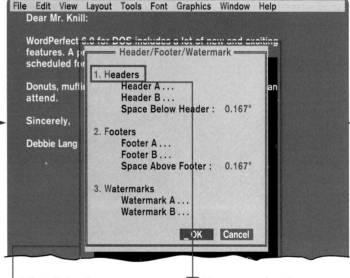

1 Position the cursor anywhere on the first page you want to include the header or footer.

2 Press `Alt` + `L` to open the **Layout** menu.

3 Press `H` to select the **Header/Footer/Watermark** command.

◆ This dialog box appears.

4 To create a header, press `H` (for **Headers**).

or

To create a footer, press `F` (for **Footers**).

Justify Text
Change Margins
Change Line Spacing
Change Tab Settings
Indent Text

Center a Page
Add Page Numbers
Add Headers or Footers
Change Paper Size and Type

TIP

◆ Your screen does not display the headers and footers, but they will appear when you print your document.

Note: To view the headers and footers in your document, refer to "Preview a Document" on page 112.

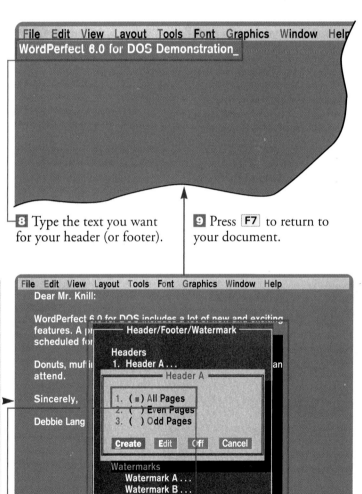

8 Type the text you want for your header (or footer).

9 Press **F7** to return to your document.

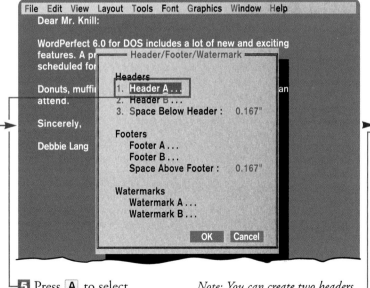

5 Press **A** to select **Header A** (or **Footer A**).

*Note: You can create two headers and two footers (**A** and **B**) for each page.*

◆ This dialog box appears.

6 Press the highlighted letter of the pages where you want the header (or footer) to appear (example: **A** for **All Pages**).

◆ A bullet appears in the brackets.

7 Press **Enter**.

CHANGE PAPER SIZE AND TYPE

WordPerfect automatically sets each page in your document to print on 8.5 by 11 inch paper. If you want to use a different size and type of paper, you can change this setting.

PAPER SIZE AND TYPE OPTIONS

Some available options are:

Envelope

Select this setting when you want to print an envelope.

Change Paper Size and Type

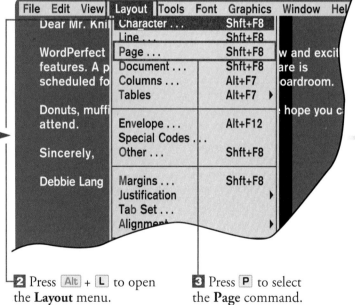

1 Position the cursor anywhere on the page you want to print on the new paper size and type.

2 Press Alt + L to open the **Layout** menu.

3 Press P to select the **Page** command.

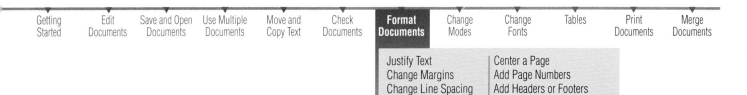

Justify Text
Change Margins
Change Line Spacing
Change Tab Settings
Indent Text

Center a Page
Add Page Numbers
Add Headers or Footers
Change Paper Size and Type

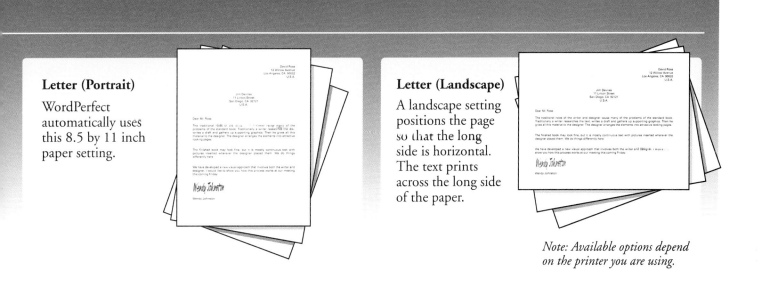

Letter (Portrait)

WordPerfect automatically uses this 8.5 by 11 inch paper setting.

Letter (Landscape)

A landscape setting positions the page so that the long side is horizontal. The text prints across the long side of the paper.

Note: Available options depend on the printer you are using.

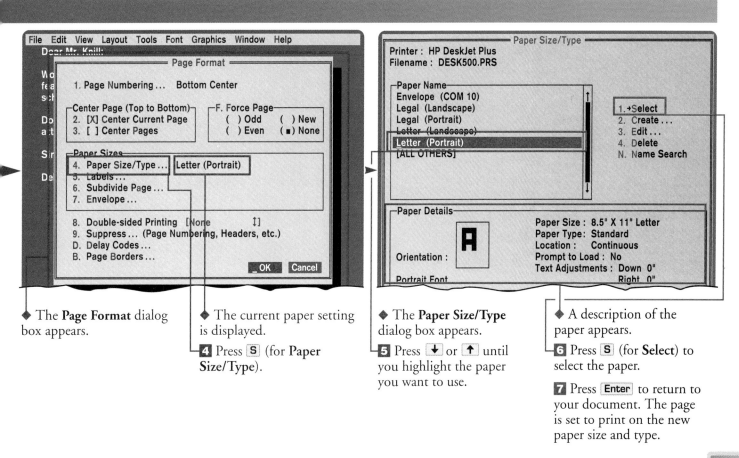

◆ The **Page Format** dialog box appears.

◆ The current paper setting is displayed.

4 Press **S** (for **Paper Size/Type**).

◆ The **Paper Size/Type** dialog box appears.

5 Press ↓ or ↑ until you highlight the paper you want to use.

◆ A description of the paper appears.

6 Press **S** (for **Select**) to select the paper.

7 Press **Enter** to return to your document. The page is set to print on the new paper size and type.

The WordPerfect Modes

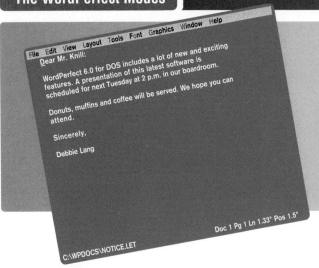

TEXT MODE

Advantages

◆ The fastest mode for entering and editing text.

◆ Requires less electronic memory than the other modes.

Disadvantages

◆ Does not show you exactly how the page will appear when you print it.

◆ Character formatting, headers, footers and graphics are not displayed on your screen.

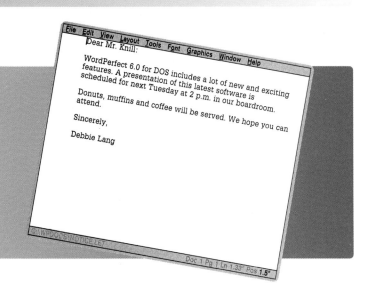

GRAPHICS MODE

Advantages

◆ Displays text and graphics on your screen as they will appear on a printed page.

◆ Offers a good environment for using the mouse.

Disadvantages

◆ Operates slower than the Text Mode.

◆ Some computers may not be able to use this mode because of hardware limitations.

PAGE MODE

Advantage

◆ Works like the Graphics Mode, but is the only mode that displays everything on the page, including headers, footers and page numbers.

Disadvantages

◆ Operates slower than the Text Mode.

◆ Some computers may not be able to use this mode because of hardware limitations.

Change to the Page Mode

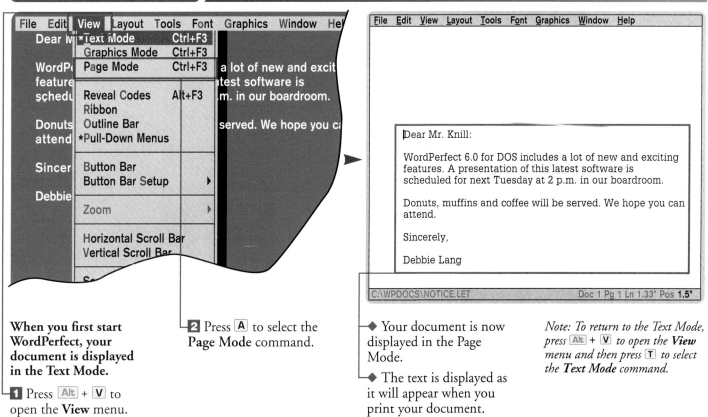

When you first start WordPerfect, your document is displayed in the Text Mode.

1 Press `Alt` + `V` to open the **View** menu.

2 Press `A` to select the **Page Mode** command.

◆ Your document is now displayed in the Page Mode.

◆ The text is displayed as it will appear when you print your document.

Note: To return to the Text Mode, press `Alt` *+* `V` *to open the* ***View*** *menu and then press* `T` *to select the* ***Text Mode*** *command.*

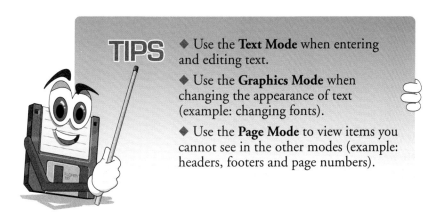

TIPS

◆ Use the **Text Mode** when entering and editing text.

◆ Use the **Graphics Mode** when changing the appearance of text (example: changing fonts).

◆ Use the **Page Mode** to view items you cannot see in the other modes (example: headers, footers and page numbers).

GRAPHICS MODE

The Graphics Mode imitates a WYSIWYG (What You See Is What You Get) environment. The document on your screen shows you almost exactly what the printed version will look like.

Change to the Graphics Mode

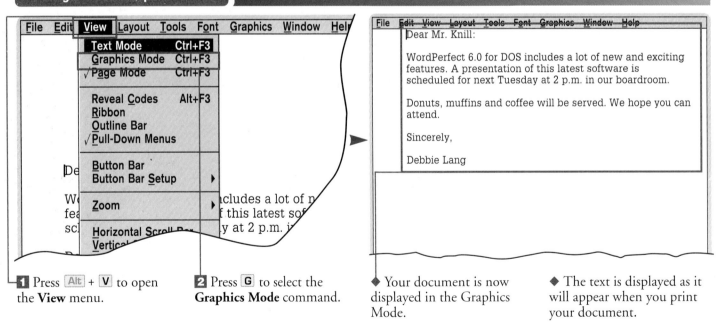

1 Press `Alt` + `V` to open the **View** menu.

2 Press `G` to select the **Graphics Mode** command.

◆ Your document is now displayed in the Graphics Mode.

◆ The text is displayed as it will appear when you print your document.

Using the Mouse

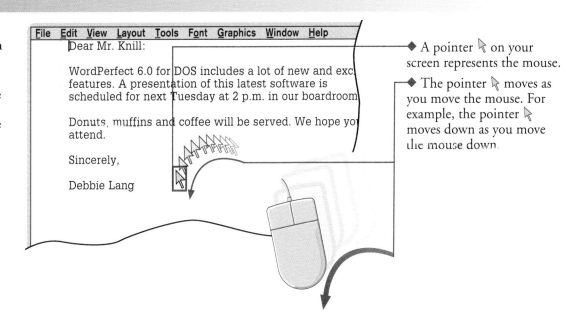

You may find it easier to use the mouse when in the Graphics or Page Mode.

You can use the mouse to open menus, select commands and choose options.

In the Graphics and Page modes, the pointer changes from ▮ to ↖.

Note: For more information on using the mouse, refer to page 6.

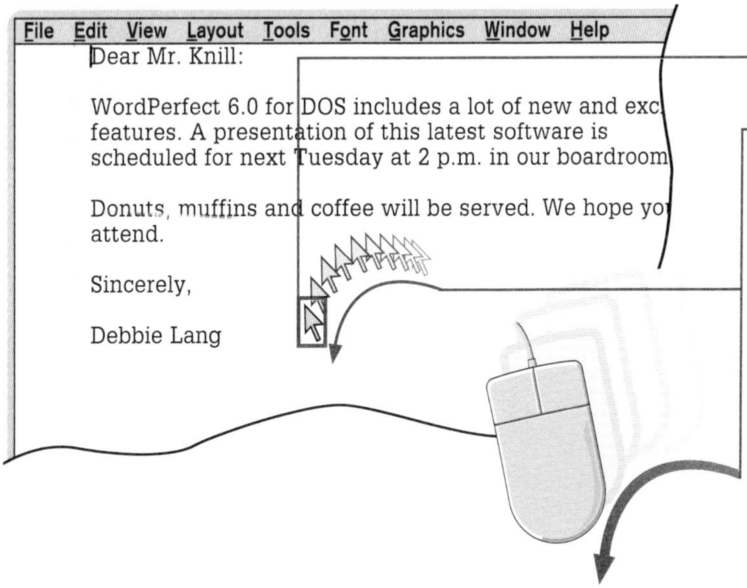

◆ A pointer ↖ on your screen represents the mouse.

◆ The pointer ↖ moves as you move the mouse. For example, the pointer ↖ moves down as you move the mouse down.

Common Commands

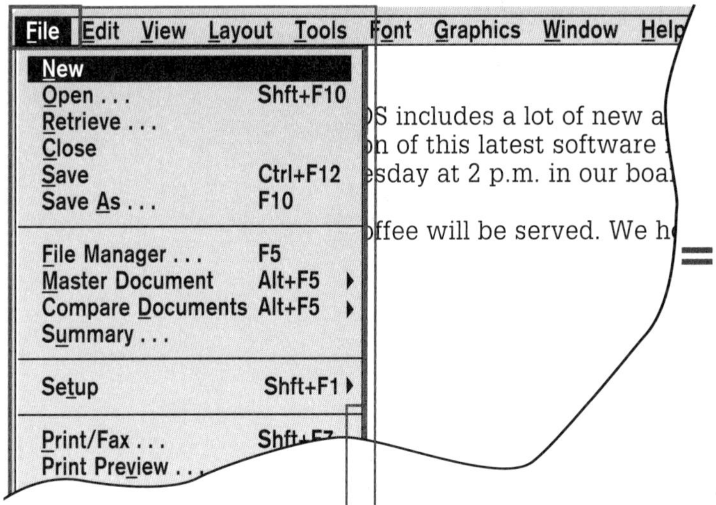

=

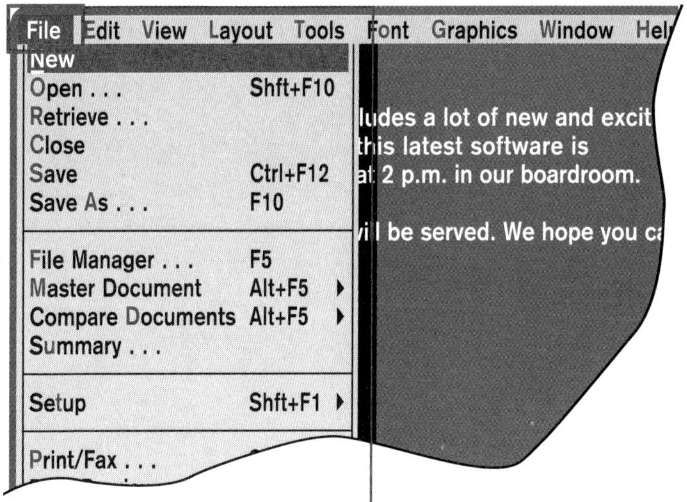

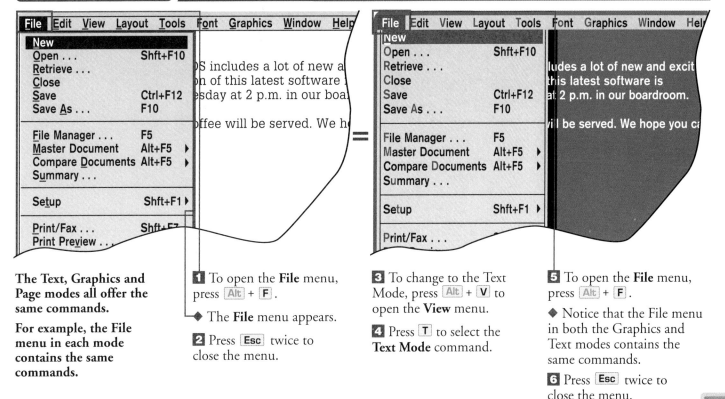

The Text, Graphics and Page modes all offer the same commands.

For example, the File menu in each mode contains the same commands.

1 To open the **File** menu, press Alt + F.

◆ The **File** menu appears.

2 Press Esc twice to close the menu.

3 To change to the Text Mode, press Alt + V to open the **View** menu.

4 Press T to select the **Text Mode** command.

5 To open the **File** menu, press Alt + F.

◆ Notice that the File menu in both the Graphics and Text modes contains the same commands.

6 Press Esc twice to close the menu.

Display the Button Bar

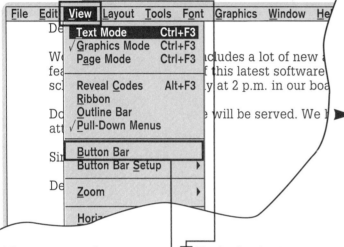

The Button Bar lets you quickly access frequently used commands.

You can only use the mouse to select a command displayed on the Button Bar.

Note: You can display the Button Bar in all modes.

For this example, it is displayed in the Graphics Mode. To change to this mode, press Alt + V *to open the* **View** *menu and then press* G *to select the* **Graphics Mode** *command.*

1 To display the Button Bar, press Alt + V to open the **View** menu.

2 Press B to select the **Button Bar** command.

◆ The Button Bar appears.

Note: To hide the Button Bar, repeat steps **1** *and* **2**.

USING THE BUTTON BAR

To select a command displayed on the Button Bar:

1 Click the button you want to select (example: **Speller**).

◆ If you click the **Speller** button, the **Speller** dialog box appears.

Note: For information on using the Speller, refer to page 64.

Speller

Speller

1. Word
2. Page
3. Document
4. From Cursor
5. Look Up Word . . .
6. Edit Supplemental Dictionary . . .

Setup . . . Shft+F1   Close

Display the Ribbon

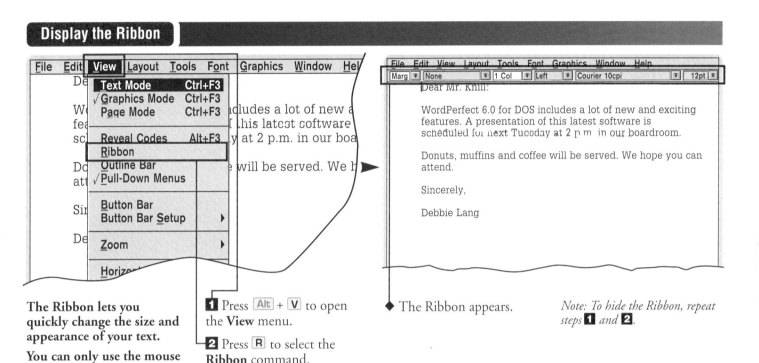

The Ribbon lets you quickly change the size and appearance of your text.

You can only use the mouse to select a feature displayed on the Ribbon.

1 Press Alt + V to open the **View** menu.

2 Press R to select the **Ribbon** command.

◆ The Ribbon appears.

Note: To hide the Ribbon, repeat steps 1 and 2.

USING THE RIBBON

To select a feature displayed on the Ribbon:

1 Block the text you want to change.

2 Click the box ▼ beside the feature you want to select.

◆ A list of options appears.

3 Double-click the option you want to use (example: **Center**).

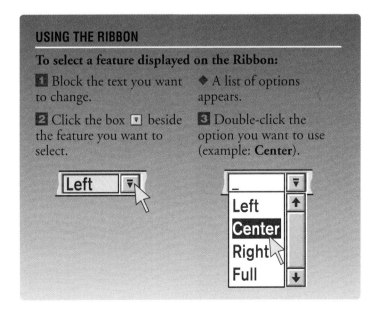

Change Text Appearance

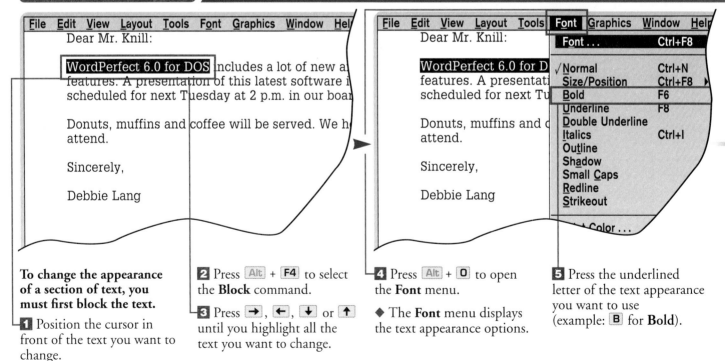

To change the appearance of a section of text, you must first block the text.

1 Position the cursor in front of the text you want to change.

2 Press `Alt` + `F4` to select the **Block** command.

3 Press `→`, `←`, `↓` or `↑` until you highlight all the text you want to change.

4 Press `Alt` + `O` to open the **Font** menu.

◆ The **Font** menu displays the text appearance options.

5 Press the underlined letter of the text appearance you want to use (example: `B` for **Bold**).

| Getting Started | Edit Documents | Save and Open Documents | Use Multiple Documents | Move and Copy Text | Check Documents | Format Documents | Change Modes | **Change Fonts** | Tables | Print Documents | Merge Documents |

Change Text Appearance
Change Fonts
Change Text Size or Position

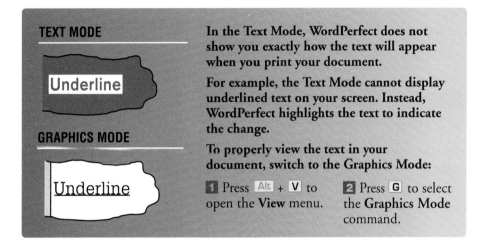

TEXT MODE

Underline

GRAPHICS MODE

Underline

In the Text Mode, WordPerfect does not show you exactly how the text will appear when you print your document.

For example, the Text Mode cannot display underlined text on your screen. Instead, WordPerfect highlights the text to indicate the change.

To properly view the text in your document, switch to the Graphics Mode:

1 Press `Alt` + `V` to open the **View** menu.

2 Press `G` to select the **Graphics Mode** command.

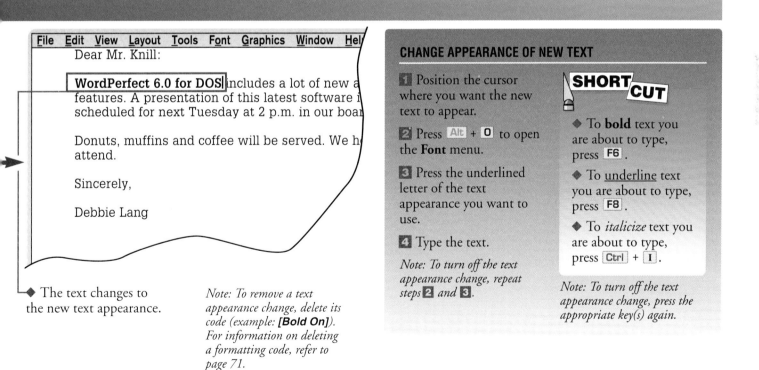

File Edit View Layout Tools Font Graphics Window Hel

Dear Mr. Knill:

WordPerfect 6.0 for DOS includes a lot of new a features. A presentation of this latest software i scheduled for next Tuesday at 2 p.m. in our boar

Donuts, muffins and coffee will be served. We h attend.

Sincerely,

Debbie Lang

◆ The text changes to the new text appearance.

Note: To remove a text appearance change, delete its code (example: **[Bold On]***). For information on deleting a formatting code, refer to page 71.*

CHANGE APPEARANCE OF NEW TEXT

1 Position the cursor where you want the new text to appear.

2 Press `Alt` + `O` to open the **Font** menu.

3 Press the underlined letter of the text appearance you want to use.

4 Type the text.

Note: To turn off the text appearance change, repeat steps **2** *and* **3**.

SHORTCUT

◆ To **bold** text you are about to type, press `F6`.

◆ To underline text you are about to type, press `F8`.

◆ To *italicize* text you are about to type, press `Ctrl` + `I`.

Note: To turn off the text appearance change, press the appropriate key(s) again.

You can change the font of the text in your document. A font refers to the design of the characters. Some examples are:

Courier
Roman
Helvetica

In the Text Mode, WordPerfect does not show you exactly how the text will appear when you print your document.

To properly view a font change, switch to the Graphics Mode:

1 Press **Alt** + **V** to open the **View** menu.

2 Press **G** to select the **Graphics Mode** command.

Change Fonts

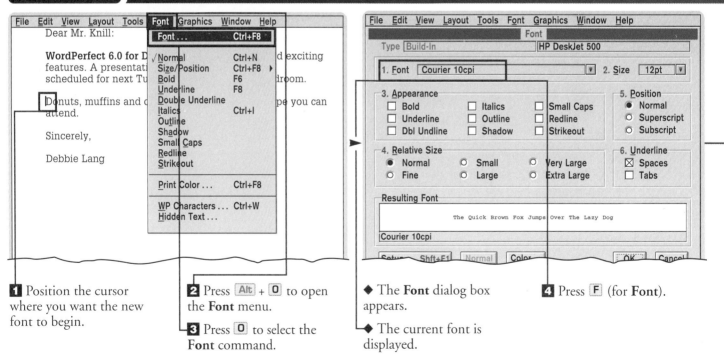

File Edit View Layout Tools **Font** Graphics Window Help

Dear Mr. Knill:

| Font... | Ctrl+F8 |

WordPerfect 6.0 for D ...d exciting
features. A presentati...
scheduled for next Tu... ...droom.

Donuts, muffins and ... ...pe you can attend.

Sincerely,

Debbie Lang

- ✓ Normal — Ctrl+N
- Size/Position — Ctrl+F8 ▶
- Bold — F6
- Underline — F8
- Double Underline
- Italics — Ctrl+I
- Outline
- Shadow
- Small Caps
- Redline
- Strikeout

Print Color... — Ctrl+F8

WP Characters... — Ctrl+W
Hidden Text...

File Edit View Layout Tools Font Graphics Window Help

Font

Type Build-In   HP DeskJet 500

1. Font Courier 10cpi   ▼   2. Size 12pt ▼

3. Appearance
- ☐ Bold   ☐ Italics   ☐ Small Caps
- ☐ Underline   ☐ Outline   ☐ Redline
- ☐ Dbl Undline ☐ Shadow   ☐ Strikeout

5. Position
- ● Normal
- ○ Superscript
- ○ Subscript

4. Relative Size
- ● Normal   ○ Small   ○ Very Large
- ○ Fine   ○ Large   ○ Extra Large

6. Underline
- ☒ Spaces
- ☐ Tabs

Resulting Font

The Quick Brown Fox Jumps Over The Lazy Dog

Courier 10cpi

Setup Shft+F1 Normal Color   OK Cancel

1 Position the cursor where you want the new font to begin.

2 Press **Alt** + **O** to open the **Font** menu.

3 Press **O** to select the **Font** command.

◆ The **Font** dialog box appears.

◆ The current font is displayed.

4 Press **F** (for **Font**).

CHANGE FONT SIZE

You can make the text in your document larger or smaller.

10 point

12 point

14 point

18 point

24 point

Note: The size of a font is measured in "points." There are 72 points per inch.

1 In the **Font** dialog box, press **S** (for **Size**).

2 Press ↓ to display the size options.

3 Press ↓ or ↑ until you highlight the size you want to use (example: **18**) and then press **Enter**.

4 Press **Enter** again to return to your document.

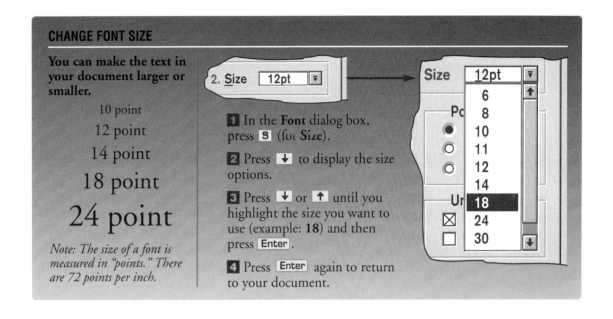

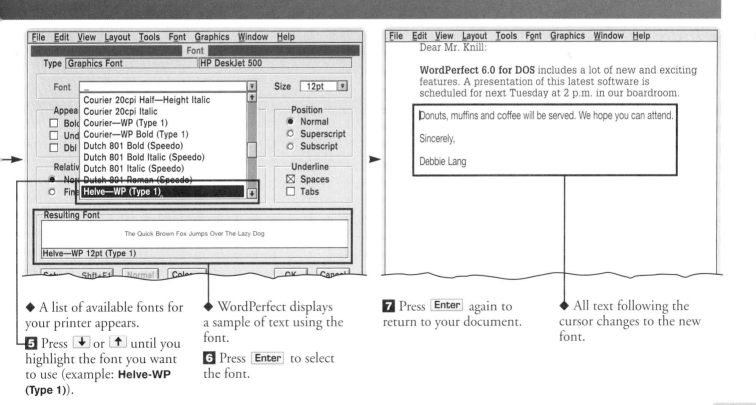

◆ A list of available fonts for your printer appears.

5 Press ↓ or ↑ until you highlight the font you want to use (example: **Helve-WP (Type 1)**).

◆ WordPerfect displays a sample of text using the font.

6 Press **Enter** to select the font.

7 Press **Enter** again to return to your document.

◆ All text following the cursor changes to the new font.

WordPerfect offers the following text size options:

Normal Size

Fine

Small

Large

Very Large

Extra Large

WordPerfect offers the following text position options:

Normal^Superscript

Normal_Subscript

Change Text Size or Position

File Edit View Layout Tools Font Graphics Window Hel

Dear Mr. Knill:

WordPerfect 6.0 for DOS includes a lot of new a features. A presentation of this latest software i scheduled for next Tuesday at 2 p.m. in our boar

Donuts, muffins and coffee will be served. We hope you can

Sincerely,

Debbie Lang

To change the size or position of a section of text, you must first block the text.

1 Position the cursor in front of the text you want to change.

2 Press `Alt` + `F4` to select the **Block** command.

3 Press `→`, `←`, `↓` or `↑` until you highlight all the text you want to change.

TEXT MODE

Extra Large_

GRAPHICS MODE

Extra Large|

In the Text Mode, WordPerfect does not show you exactly how the text will appear when you print your document.

For example, the Text Mode cannot display extra large text on your screen. Instead, WordPerfect highlights the text to indicate the change.

To properly view the text in your document, switch to the Graphics Mode:

1 Press `Alt` + `V` to open the **View** menu.

2 Press `G` to select the **Graphics Mode** command.

| Getting Started | Edit Documents | Save and Open Documents | Use Multiple Documents | Move and Copy Text | Check Documents | Format Documents | Change Modes | **Change Fonts** | Tables | Print Documents | Merge Documents |

Change Text Appearance
Change Fonts
Change Text Size or Position

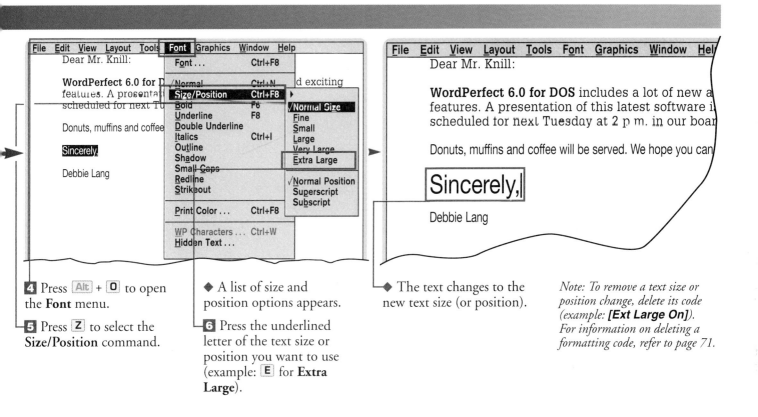

4 Press Alt + O to open the **Font** menu.

5 Press Z to select the **Size/Position** command.

◆ A list of size and position options appears.

6 Press the underlined letter of the text size or position you want to use (example: E for **Extra Large**).

◆ The text changes to the new text size (or position).

Note: To remove a text size or position change, delete its code (example: [Ext Large On]). For information on deleting a formatting code, refer to page 71.

CHANGE SIZE OF NEW TEXT

1 Position the cursor where you want the new text to appear.

2 Press Alt + O to open the **Font** menu.

3 Press Z to select the **Size/Position** command.

4 Press the underlined letter of the text size you want to use.

5 Type the text.

*Note: To turn off the text size change, repeat steps 2 and 3, then press Z (for **Normal Size**).*

CREATE
A TABLE

A table helps you organize information into rows and columns.

Create a Table

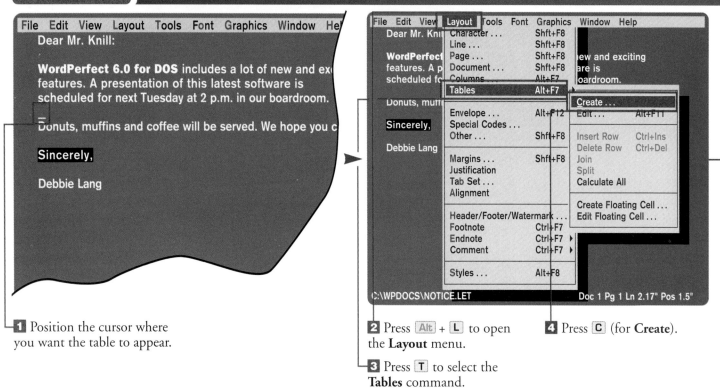

1 Position the cursor where you want the table to appear.

2 Press Alt + L to open the **Layout** menu.

3 Press T to select the **Tables** command.

4 Press C (for **Create**).

A table consists of rows, columns and cells.

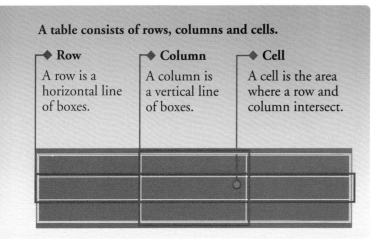

◆ Row

A row is a horizontal line of boxes.

◆ Column

A column is a vertical line of boxes.

◆ Cell

A cell is the area where a row and column intersect.

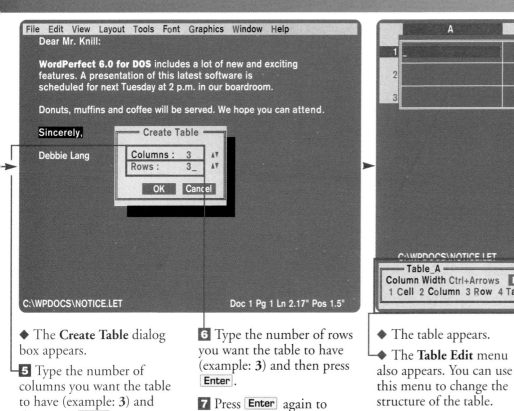

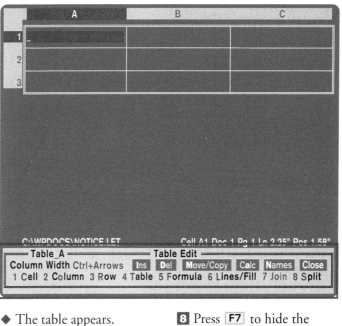

◆ The **Create Table** dialog box appears.

5 Type the number of columns you want the table to have (example: **3**) and then press **Enter**.

6 Type the number of rows you want the table to have (example: **3**) and then press **Enter**.

7 Press **Enter** again to create the table.

◆ The table appears.

◆ The **Table Edit** menu also appears. You can use this menu to change the structure of the table.

8 Press **F7** to hide the **Table Edit** menu and return to your document.

TYPE TEXT

CHANGE COLUMN WIDTH

You can type text into each cell in a table. To accommodate the amount of text you type, WordPerfect automatically adjusts the height of the row for you. You can adjust the columns to make them wider or narrower.

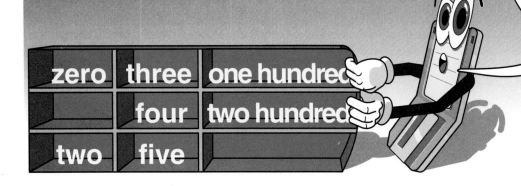

Type Text in a Table

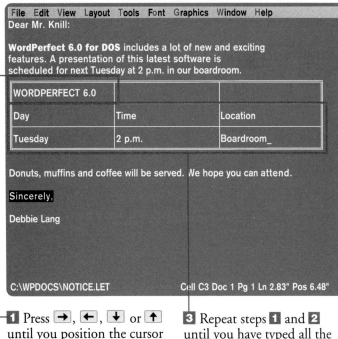

1 Press →, ←, ↓ or ↑ until you position the cursor in the cell where you want to type text.

2 Type the text.

*Note: You cannot type text in a table when the **Table Edit** menu is displayed.*

3 Repeat steps **1** and **2** until you have typed all the text.

Change Column Width

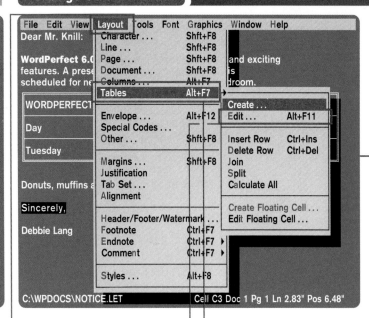

To change a column width in a table, you must first display the Table Edit menu.

1 Press Alt + L to open the **Layout** menu.

2 Press T to select the **Tables** command.

3 Press E (for **Edit**).

Create a Table
Type Text
Change Column Width
Add a Row or Column
Join Cells
Change Table Lines

TIPS

◆ To quickly display the **Table Edit** menu, press `Alt` + `F11`.

◆ To hide the **Table Edit** menu and return to your document, press `F7`.

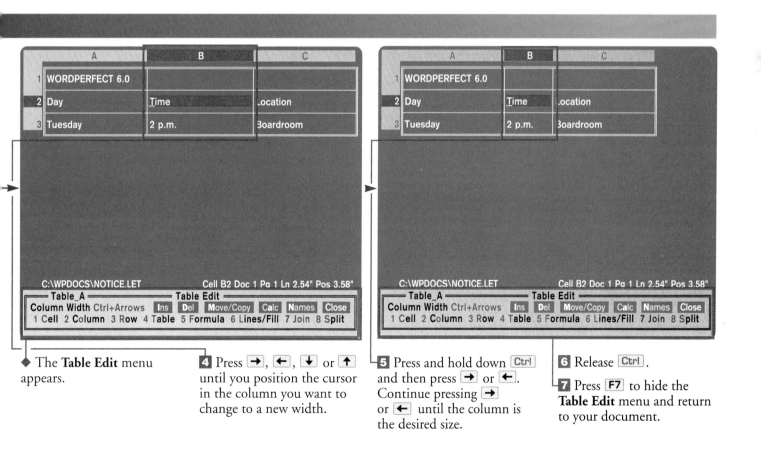

◆ The **Table Edit** menu appears.

4 Press `→`, `←`, `↓` or `↑` until you position the cursor in the column you want to change to a new width.

5 Press and hold down `Ctrl` and then press `→` or `←`. Continue pressing `→` or `←` until the column is the desired size.

6 Release `Ctrl`.

7 Press `F7` to hide the **Table Edit** menu and return to your document.

ADD A ROW
OR COLUMN

You can add a row or column to a table.

Add a Row or Column

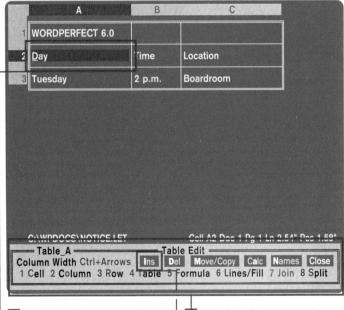

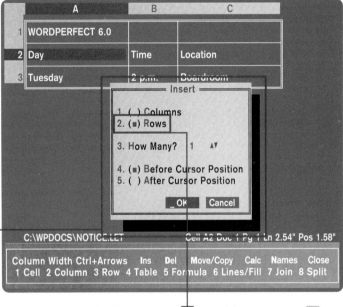

1 Position the cursor where you want to add a row or column.

2 Display the **Table Edit** menu.

*Note: To quickly display the **Table Edit** menu, press* Alt *+* F11 *.*

3 Press I (for **Insert**).

◆ The **Insert** dialog box appears.

4 To add a row, press R (for **Rows**).

or

To add a column, press C (for **Columns**).

Note: To add more than one row or column, press H *(for **How Many?**), type the number you want to add and then press* Enter *.*

Create a Table
Type Text
Change Column Width
Add a Row or Column
Join Cells
Change Table Lines

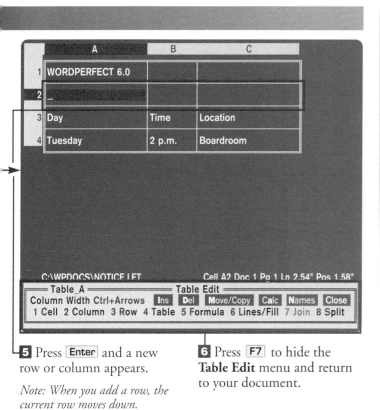

5 Press `Enter` and a new row or column appears.

Note: When you add a row, the current row moves down.

When you add a column, the current column moves to the right.

6 Press `F7` to hide the **Table Edit** menu and return to your document.

DELETE A ROW OR COLUMN

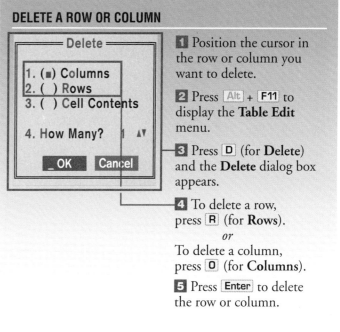

1 Position the cursor in the row or column you want to delete.

2 Press `Alt` + `F11` to display the **Table Edit** menu.

3 Press `D` (for **Delete**) and the **Delete** dialog box appears.

4 To delete a row, press `R` (for **Rows**).
or
To delete a column, press `O` (for **Columns**).

5 Press `Enter` to delete the row or column.

You can combine two or more cells to make one large cell.

Join Cells

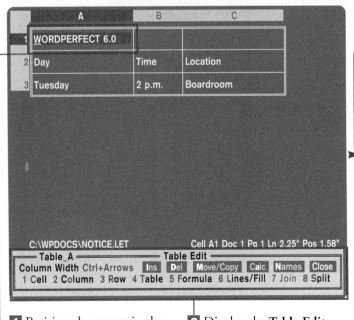

1 Position the cursor in the first cell you want to join with other cells.

2 Display the **Table Edit** menu.

*Note: To quickly display the **Table Edit** menu, press* Alt + F11 .

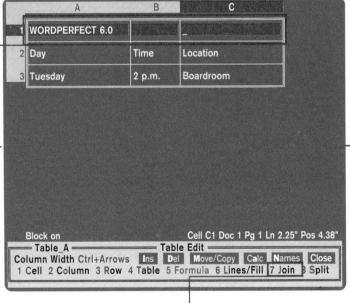

3 To indicate which cells you want to join, press Alt + F4 to select the **Block** command.

4 Press → or ↓ until you highlight the cells you want to join together.

5 Press J (for **Join**).

SPLIT CELLS

You can split one cell into two or more cells.

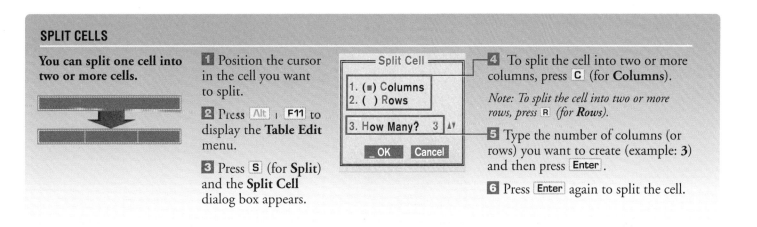

1 Position the cursor in the cell you want to split.

2 Press `Alt` + `F11` to display the **Table Edit** menu.

3 Press `S` (for **Split**) and the **Split Cell** dialog box appears.

— Split Cell —

1. (■) Columns
2. ( ) Rows

3. How Many?   3 ▲▼

_ OK   Cancel

4 To split the cell into two or more columns, press `C` (for **Columns**).

Note: To split the cell into two or more rows, press `R` (for Rows).

5 Type the number of columns (or rows) you want to create (example: **3**) and then press `Enter`.

6 Press `Enter` again to split the cell.

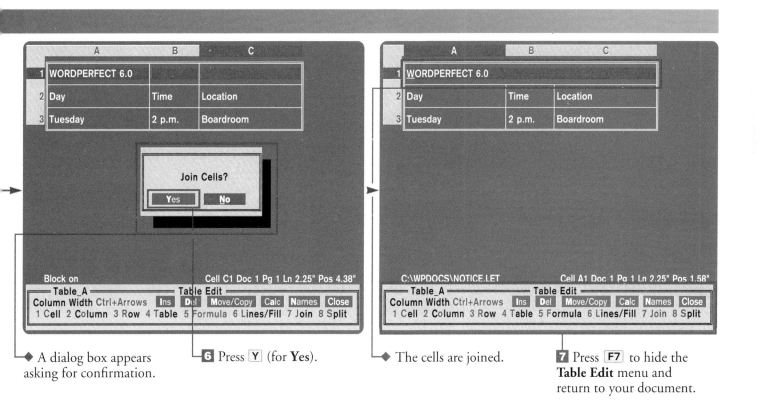

◆ A dialog box appears asking for confirmation.

6 Press `Y` (for **Yes**).

◆ The cells are joined.

7 Press `F7` to hide the **Table Edit** menu and return to your document.

You can change the type of lines used in a table. Some examples are:

Single	———————————
Double	═══════════
Dashed	– – – – – – –
Dotted	·············
Thick	———————————
Extra Thick	═══════════

Change Table Lines

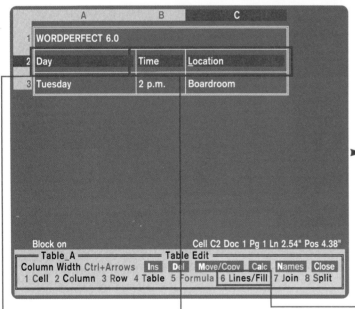

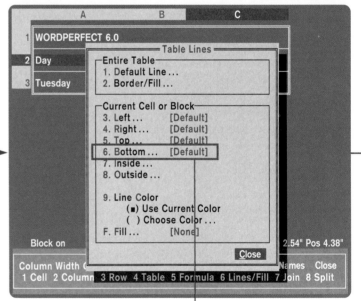

1 Position the cursor in the first cell you want to change.

2 Display the **Table Edit** menu.

Note: To quickly display the Table Edit menu, press Alt + F11 .

3 To indicate which cells you want to change, press Alt + F4 to select the **Block** command.

4 Press →, ←, ↓ or ↑ until you highlight the cells you want to change.

5 Press L (for **Lines/Fill**).

◆ The **Table Lines** dialog box appears. It contains a list of lines you can change.

6 Press the highlighted letter of the line you want to change (example: B for **Bottom**).

Getting Started	Edit Documents	Save and Open Documents	Use Multiple Documents	Move and Copy Text	Check Documents	Format Documents	Change Modes	Change Fonts	**Tables**	Print Documents	Merge Documents

Create a Table
Type Text
Change Column Width
Add a Row or Column
Join Cells
Change Table Lines

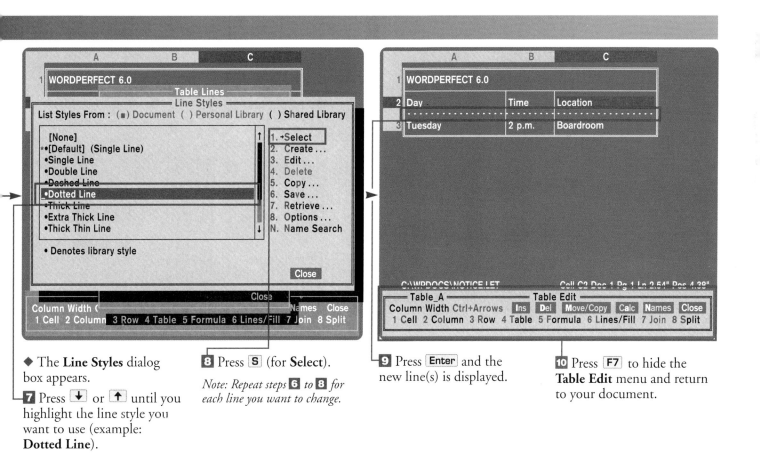

◆ The **Line Styles** dialog box appears.

7 Press ↓ or ↑ until you highlight the line style you want to use (example: **Dotted Line**).

8 Press **S** (for **Select**).

Note: Repeat steps 6 to 8 for each line you want to change.

9 Press **Enter** and the new line(s) is displayed.

10 Press **F7** to hide the **Table Edit** menu and return to your document.

PREVIEW A DOCUMENT

> You can use the Print Preview command to see what your document will look like before you actually print it.

Preview Your Document

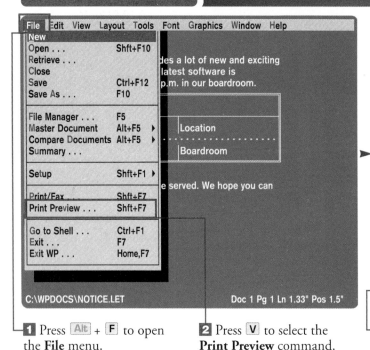

1 Press `Alt` + `F` to open the **File** menu.

2 Press `V` to select the **Print Preview** command.

◆ WordPerfect displays the document on your screen exactly the way it will look when you print it.

Note: You cannot edit your document.

Change Magnification

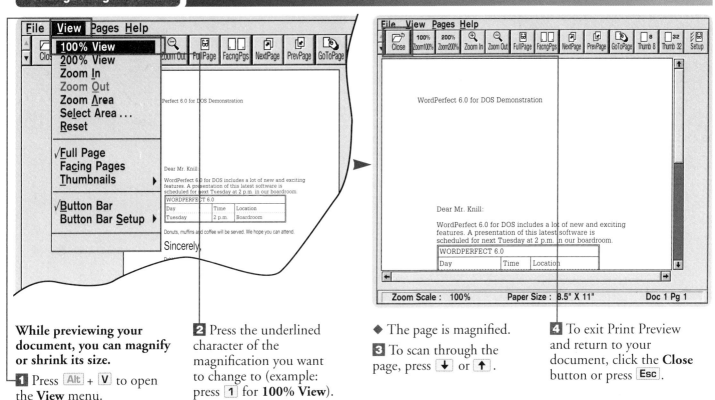

While previewing your document, you can magnify or shrink its size.

1 Press `Alt` + `V` to open the **View** menu.

2 Press the underlined character of the magnification you want to change to (example: press `1` for **100% View**).

◆ The page is magnified.

3 To scan through the page, press `↓` or `↑`.

4 To exit Print Preview and return to your document, click the **Close** button or press `Esc`.

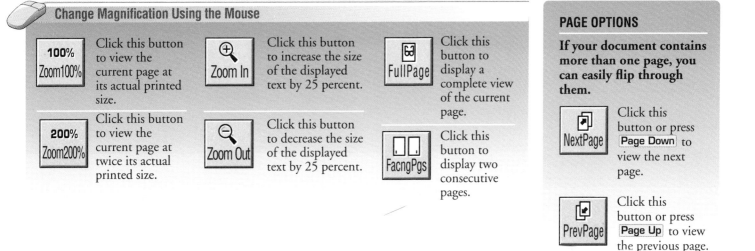

Change Magnification Using the Mouse

100% Zoom100% Click this button to view the current page at its actual printed size.

200% Zoom200% Click this button to view the current page at twice its actual printed size.

Zoom In Click this button to increase the size of the displayed text by 25 percent.

Zoom Out Click this button to decrease the size of the displayed text by 25 percent.

FullPage Click this button to display a complete view of the current page.

FacngPgs Click this button to display two consecutive pages.

PAGE OPTIONS

If your document contains more than one page, you can easily flip through them.

NextPage Click this button or press `Page Down` to view the next page.

PrevPage Click this button or press `Page Up` to view the previous page.

113

PRINT A DOCUMENT

You can print a single page, specific pages or your entire document.

Print Your Entire Document

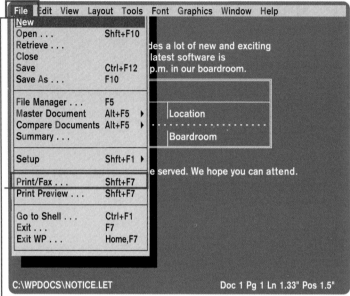

| File | Edit | View | Layout | Tools | Font | Graphics | Window | Help |

New
Open . . .   Shft+F10
Retrieve . . .
Close
Save   Ctrl+F12
Save As . . .   F10

File Manager . . .   F5
Master Document   Alt+F5 ▶
Compare Documents Alt+F5 ▶
Summary . . .

Setup   Shft+F1 ▶

Print/Fax . . .   Shft+F7
Print Preview . . .   Shft+F7

Go to Shell . . .   Ctrl+F1
Exit . . .   F7
Exit WP . . .   Home,F7

des a lot of new and exciting
latest software is
p.m. in our boardroom.

Location

Boardroom

e served. We hope you can attend.

C:\WPDOCS\NOTICE.LET   Doc 1 Pg 1 Ln 1.33" Pos 1.5"

1 Press **Alt** + **F** to open the **File** menu.

2 Press **P** to select the **Print/Fax** command.

Press **Shift** + **F7**.

| Getting Started | Edit Documents | Save and Open Documents | Use Multiple Documents | Move and Copy Text | Check Documents | Format Documents | Change Modes | Change Fonts | Tables | **Print Documents** | Merge Documents |

Preview a Document
Print a Document

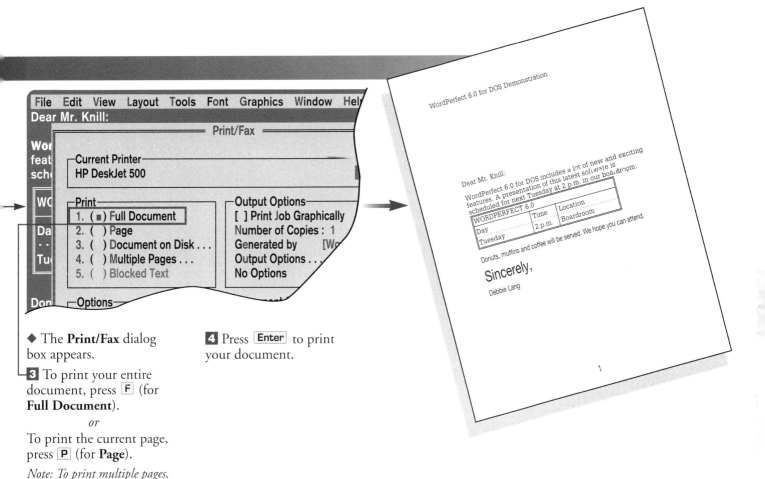

◆ The **Print/Fax** dialog box appears.

3 To print your entire document, press **F** (for **Full Document**).

or

To print the current page, press **P** (for **Page**).

Note: To print multiple pages, see below.

4 Press **Enter** to print your document.

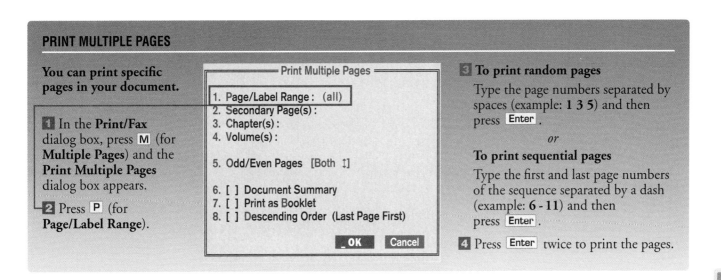

PRINT MULTIPLE PAGES

You can print specific pages in your document.

1 In the **Print/Fax** dialog box, press **M** (for **Multiple Pages**) and the **Print Multiple Pages** dialog box appears.

2 Press **P** (for **Page/Label Range**).

3 To print random pages

Type the page numbers separated by spaces (example: **1 3 5**) and then press **Enter**.

or

To print sequential pages

Type the first and last page numbers of the sequence separated by a dash (example: **6 - 11**) and then press **Enter**.

4 Press **Enter** twice to print the pages.

You can use the Merge feature to automate the process of sending a personalized letter to a large group of people.

Form File

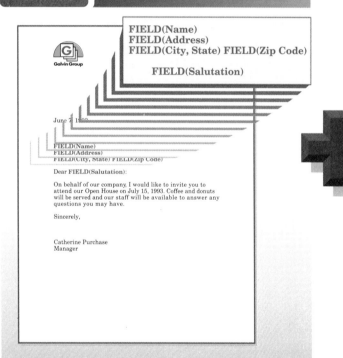

FIELD(Name)
FIELD(Address)
FIELD(City, State) FIELD(Zip Code)

FIELD(Salutation)

June 7, 1993

FIELD(Name)
FIELD(Address)
FIELD(City, State) FIELD(Zip Code)

Dear FIELD(Salutation):

On behalf of our company, I would like to invite you to attend our Open House on July 15, 1993. Coffee and donuts will be served and our staff will be available to answer any questions you may have.

Sincerely,

Catherine Purchase
Manager

A Form file contains the text that will appear in each letter. It also contains FIELD codes that tell WordPerfect where to insert the personalized information that changes from letter to letter.

Data File

○ **Record 3** ○
FIELD(Name): **Mr. David Ross**
(Address): **12 Willow Avenue**
CA

○ **Record 2** ○
FIELD(Name): **Mrs. Heather Matwey**
(Address): **56 Devon Road**
CA

○ **Record 1** ○
FIELD(Name): **Mr. John Smith**
FIELD(Address): **11 Linton Street**
FIELD(City, State): **Atlanta, GA**
FIELD(Zip Code): **30367**
FIELD(Salutation): **Mr. Smith**

A Data file contains the information for each person you want to send the letter to (example: names, addresses).

The information for each person is called a **record**.

The information within each record is broken down into **fields**.

Getting Started | Edit Documents | Save and Open Documents | Use Multiple Documents | Move and Copy Text | Check Documents | Format Documents | Change Modes | Change Fonts | Tables | Print Documents | **Merge Documents**

Introduction
Create a Data File
Create a Form File
Merge Files

Merged File

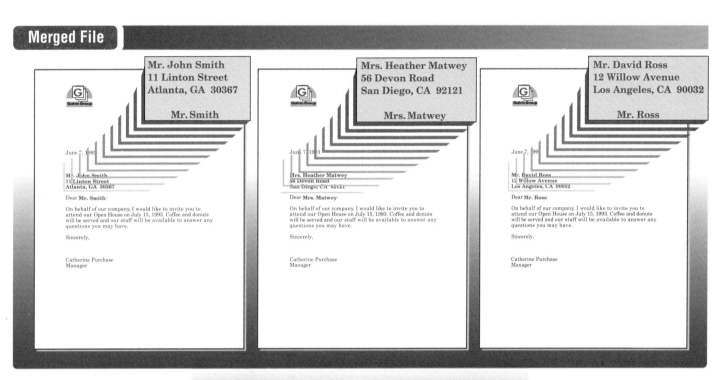

This file is the result of merging the Form and Data files.

WordPerfect inserts the personalized information from the Data file into the Form file.

Create a Data File

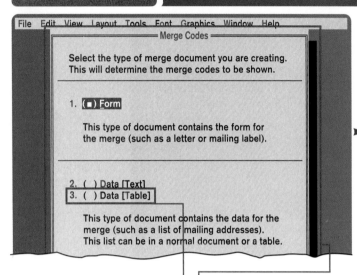

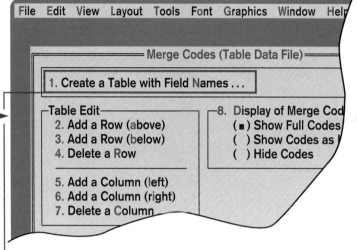

You must tell WordPerfect you are creating a Data file before you can begin working on it.

Note: To open a new document, press Alt *+* F *to open the* **File** *menu and then press* N *to select the* **New** *command.*

1 Press Shift + F9 and the **Merge Codes** dialog box appears. It asks you to select the type of merge document you are creating.

2 Press T to select the **Data [Table]** option.

3 Press N (for **Create a Table with Field Names**).

Enter Data

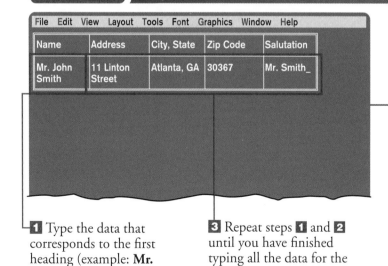

1 Type the data that corresponds to the first heading (example: **Mr. John Smith**).

2 Press Tab to move to the next cell.

3 Repeat steps **1** and **2** until you have finished typing all the data for the customer.

Getting Started | Edit Documents | Save and Open Documents | Use Multiple Documents | Move and Copy Text | Check Documents | Format Documents | Change Modes | Change Fonts | Tables | Print Documents | **Merge Documents**

Introduction
Create a Data File
Create a Form File
Merge Files

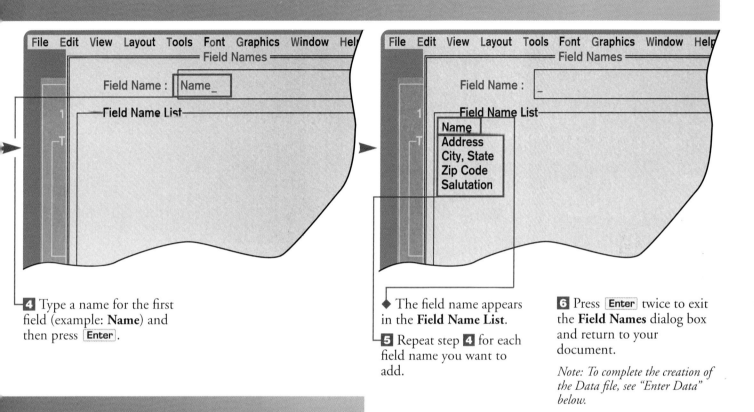

File Edit View Layout Tools Font Graphics Window Help
─────── Field Names ───────
Field Name : |Name_|
─Field Name List─

File Edit View Layout Tools Font Graphics Window Help
─────── Field Names ───────
Field Name : |_|
─Field Name List─
Name
Address
City, State
Zip Code
Salutation

4 Type a name for the first field (example: **Name**) and then press Enter.

◆ The field name appears in the **Field Name List**.

5 Repeat step **4** for each field name you want to add.

6 Press Enter twice to exit the **Field Names** dialog box and return to your document.

Note: To complete the creation of the Data file, see "Enter Data" below.

File Edit View Layout Tools Font Graphics Window Help

Name	Address	City, State	Zip Code	Salutation
Mr. John Smith	11 Linton Street	Atlanta, GA	30367	Mr. Smith
Mrs. Heather Matwey	56 Devon Road	San Diego, CA	92121	Mrs. Matwey
Mr. David Ross	12 Willow Avenue	Los Angeles, CA	90032	Mr. Ross_

4 Press Tab to add a new row.

Note: Although some text you type may not fit on one line in the table, it will print on one line in the final merge document.

5 Repeat steps **1** to **4** for each customer.

6 To save the Data file, press F10, type a name for your document (example: **CUSTOMER**) and then press Enter.

A Form file contains the text that will appear in each letter. It also contains codes that tell WordPerfect where to insert the information from a Data file.

Create a Form File

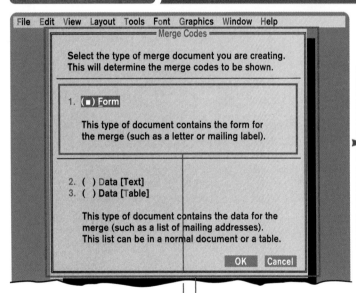

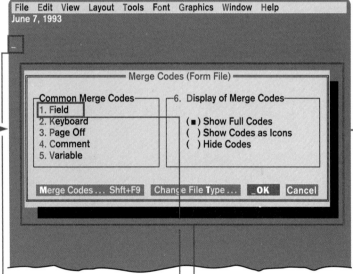

You must tell WordPerfect you are creating a Form file before you can begin working on it.

Note: To open a new document, press Alt *+* F *to open the **File** menu and then press* N *to select the **New** command.*

1 Press Shift + F9 and the **Merge Codes** dialog box appears. It asks you to select the type of merge document you are creating.

2 Press Enter to select the **Form** option.

3 Press Enter again to return to your document.

4 Begin typing the letter as you would any WordPerfect document.

5 When you reach the part of the letter where you want to insert information from a data file, press Shift + F9.

◆ The **Merge Codes (Form File)** dialog box appears.

6 Press F (for **Field**).

Getting Started   Edit Documents   Save and Open Documents   Use Multiple Documents   Move and Copy Text   Check Documents   Format Documents   Change Modes   Change Fonts   Tables   Print Documents   **Merge Documents**

Introduction
Create a Data File
Create a Form File
Merge Files

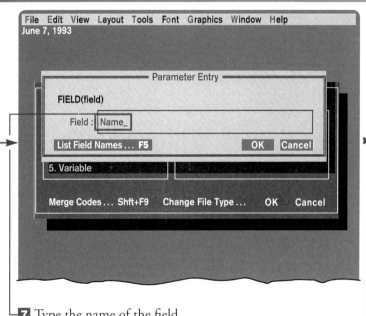

7 Type the name of the field you want to insert (example: **Name**) and then press **Enter**.

◆ A code appears on your screen (example: **FIELD(Name)**).

◆ To start a new line, press **Enter**.

8 Continue typing the letter, repeating steps **5** to **7** for each field you want to insert.

9 To save the Form file, press **F10**, type a name for your document (example: **LETTER**) and then press **Enter**.

MERGE
FILES

You can merge the Form and Data files to personalize a standard letter for several people.

Merge Files

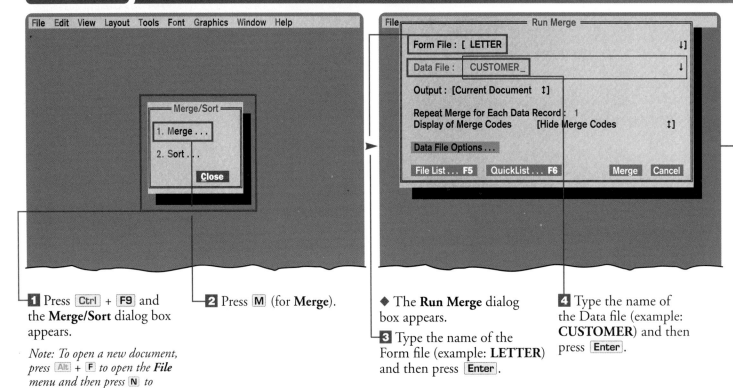

1 Press **Ctrl** + **F9** and the **Merge/Sort** dialog box appears.

Note: To open a new document, press **Alt** + **F** *to open the* **File** *menu and then press* **N** *to select the* **New** *command.*

2 Press **M** (for **Merge**).

◆ The **Run Merge** dialog box appears.

3 Type the name of the Form file (example: **LETTER**) and then press **Enter**.

4 Type the name of the Data file (example: **CUSTOMER**) and then press **Enter**.

USING MERGE TO CREATE ENVELOPES

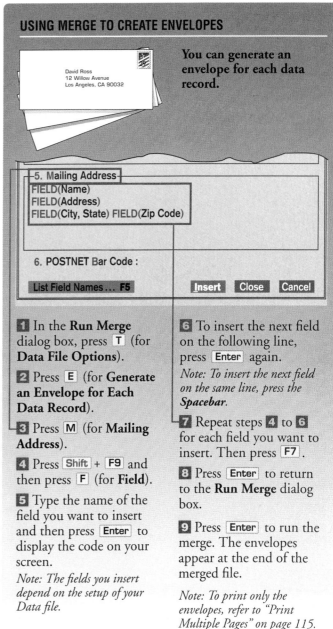

You can generate an envelope for each data record.

1 In the **Run Merge** dialog box, press **T** (for **Data File Options**).

2 Press **E** (for **Generate an Envelope for Each Data Record**).

3 Press **M** (for **Mailing Address**).

4 Press **Shift** + **F9** and then press **F** (for **Field**).

5 Type the name of the field you want to insert and then press **Enter** to display the code on your screen.

Note: The fields you insert depend on the setup of your Data file.

6 To insert the next field on the following line, press **Enter** again.

*Note: To insert the next field on the same line, press the **Spacebar**.*

7 Repeat steps **4** to **6** for each field you want to insert. Then press **F7**.

8 Press **Enter** to return to the **Run Merge** dialog box.

9 Press **Enter** to run the merge. The envelopes appear at the end of the merged file.

Note: To print only the envelopes, refer to "Print Multiple Pages" on page 115.

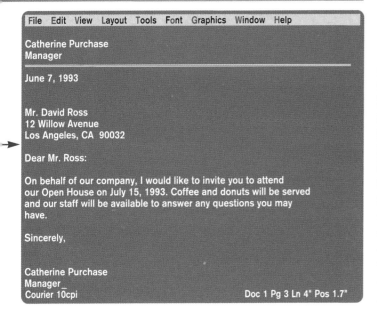

5 Press **Enter** again to merge the files.

6 Press **↑** to scroll through the document to ensure no errors have occurred.

◆ You can edit and print this document as you would any WordPerfect document.

Note: To conserve hard drive space, you do not have to save the merged document after you print it.